BREATH
IN OUR LUNGS

HOW GOD'S SPIRIT HEALS
OUR IMPERFECT STORIES

CHRISTINE COWN

Breath in Our Lungs: How God's Spirit Heals Our Imperfect Stories -
Copyright ® 2025 by Christine Cown
Published by UNITED HOUSE Publishing

All rights reserved. No portion of this book may be reproduced or shared in any form - electronic, printed, photocopied, recording, or by any information storage or retrieval system, without prior written permission from the publisher. The use of short quotations is permitted.

All Scripture quotations, unless otherwise indicated, are taken from the Holy Bible, New International Version®, NIV®. Copyright ©1973, 1978, 1984, 2011 by Biblica, Inc.™ Used by permission of Zondervan. All rights reserved worldwide. www.zondervan.comThe "NIV" and "New International Version" are trademarks registered in the United States Patent and Trademark Office by Biblica, Inc.™
Fitzgerald, F. Scott. 2013. The Great Gatsby. Harlow, England: Penguin Books.

ISBN - 978-1-952840-64-7

UNITED HOUSE Publishing Clarkston, Michigan
info@unitedhousepublishing.com www.unitedhousepublishing.com

Photography: Jenna Pelletier
Cover & Interior Design: Talitha McGuinness; talitha@unitedhousepublishing.com

Printed in the United States of America 2025 - First Edition

SPECIAL SALES
Most UNITED HOUSE books are available at special quantity discounts when purchased in bulk by corporations, organizations, and special interest groups. For more information, please email orders@unitedhousepublishing.com.

DEDICATION

To my daughter, Josephine, and the many other courageous, vulnerable women whose paths have led me to share my story. May we continue to stand on one another's shoulders to cultivate generations who will not be silenced. And to the brave men who choose to listen.

Breath in Our Lungs is a work of nonfiction. Dialogue, names, and identifying details have been changed.

The umbilical cord was wrapped around my neck the day Mom exhaled me into this world, and I have been learning to breathe ever since. Looking back, I see the long strand of broken pearls that brought me here. From conception, my days spoke of subtle discontent. While I was still in the womb, Mom wept endlessly. She grieved, tormented by my existence, as her belly swelled with unfolding life. Mom hid her form from my father; fearful and alone, she waited in the darkness of her secrecy until her body gave her away. The potential of having a little boy after two girls would certainly assuage the news of an unforeseen third pregnancy. In desperate hope, my parents named me Seth Michael pre-birth. If only I had been born male, we all would have sighed in relief. Exhausted from labor, Mom chose surgery; without a word from Mom to anyone, the doctor wheeled her into a room where the choice to create life again was permanently finished. "Christine," meaning "Christ-like," became my name scribbled on a birth certificate. Despite the circumstances, my name was written from the earth's foundations, proving God wins even when victory is not readily seen.

With each passing birthday, the family gathered around the table, where candles were lit, on a pile of homemade chocolate frosting. Mom always guided the conversation to my birth, with the best intention of highlighting the good and illuminating the darkness. Without realizing the full weight of the implications surrounding my conception and birth, I had worn laughing labels of "ugly child," "Seth Michael," and "afterthought." I developed an unhealthy view of myself, which led to confused thoughts about sexuality, my body, and the idea I could be created in the image of God. I grew to assume that even in my most intimate relationships, people would ultimately reject me, leaving me feeling hopelessly abandoned, even when connected to others. An inner critic developed with the gnawing accusation that I deserved no love, affirmation, or acceptance, and it chided me throughout childhood, seamlessly weaving into the fabric of adolescent life. I began to relate to others through mostly fear and shame. Without my awareness, these emotions grew rooted in my identity.

Having grown up in the church, I always knew about God. However, my theology proved less than foundational to my faith. God stood in the form of a stern father, much like my own. Jesus came and wrapped his arms around me and told me everything would work out if I followed the rules. The Holy Spirit was the warm feeling I experienced internally when I sang songs on Sunday mornings. Believing only these things about the character of the Trinity, I was unprepared for the emotions and questions that came later in life when family revealed its true form, relationships backlashed, and Christianity became empty. They no longer offered comfort.

John's gospel hopes that Jesus came into the world so "[we] may have life, and have it to the full[est]." In the previous sentence, however, we are reminded, "The thief comes only to steal and kill and destroy" (John 10:10). I was unaware of the devil's schemes, and the deceit of the enemy choked out the truth of my identity in Christ, allowing for all kinds of evil to manifest. The enemy's lies can only be defeated when we *believe* we have an enemy. For too many years, I felt like I was walking around with my shoelaces untied, stumbling through my days. I chose to believe my worth was wrapped up in being good rather than because I was loved.

And so, the unfolding began. God whispered to me many times throughout the years, chiseling away at false notions of abundant life apart from God and why I exist. The dust settled on my fierce autonomy, days spent disregarding God's voice. When I slipped into a quiet space, there was where God, again, found me. He broke through the veil to loudly speak purpose.

Tell your story, God invited. *Tell your story.*

"But, God . . ." I stammered. Like Moses struck by the burning bush fire, I disregarded Holy Ground. Most of my days comprised "but, God" moments, exposing my independence. More than a decade after the initial invitation to share my story, I was still painfully unaware of His sovereignty. I stumbled again: "Lord, I have no story to tell." I held up poster children of Christianity, lives birthing fruit I was confident I did not possess. "Choose them!" The envy runs thick and deep. The hiss of the deceiver echoed in my ear.

"I have no story," I protested.

But, oh. His unavoidable whisper: *This is My story. You hinder My glory when you hide under your scars.*

There are two common ways to view a piece of art. Some, like my husband, want the details. They want to understand the context, the purpose behind the artist's creation, what process was administered for it to materialize, and the ability to count each stroke. Others, like me, simply want to take a step back to appreciate and enjoy the fullness of the emotion on display, letting the piece speak of the artist's humanity. The stories of our lives are a work of art; we are masterpieces. Therefore, we must learn to look back at the sometimes painful details with compassionate curiosity to participate in the fullness of the present. We view the circumstances of our relational history to delight in the people we are today. Owning our stories is an invitation to step into true healing. Each act of forgiveness is a seal of gold on the cracks within the clay, strengthening the broken pieces of our past. I hope the risk of this vulnerable offering will give you permission to search your story and move forward so you can stay awake to the wonder of your one wild and extraordinary life.

Here I am, Lord, exposing my scars. May You have all the glory.

Christine

Chapter 1

Fear entered my dreams, melding itself to my bones. I pulled the covers over my neck and clenched my eyes into tiny slits. The scratchy cut-outs of the eyelet sheet scraped gently under my chin. Dad was yelling again. The light created a sliver through the crack in the door and traveled across the smooth wooden floor. I could barely make out the grooves of pine where knots flattened out into sturdy beams, only to be trampled upon by the thundering feet that stomped outside the door. The imperfections where the branches once grew formed the eyes of monsters, each with distinct mouths and tongues. Their eyes were wide and waiting.

Words from Dad, too overwhelming for my young mind to comprehend, made their way through my skin and into my heart, where they remained and became dormant. In the space between screams, I noticed tiny fragments of my breath. In and out. Vapors warmed the top of the blue and white fabric where ducks walked gingerly across the bedspread. Then came the piercing silence. Nothing resolved, yet nothing to be said. An awful quiet filled the space. There's only room for me to remain unnoticed. I lay in my bed in thinning *Beauty and the Beast* pajamas. Tears blazed across my cheek and seared the black thread that crossed back and forth, detailing Cinnamon Bear's triangular nose. I snuggled his worn fur, wanting so badly for someone to reach through the covers, pull them back, and expose my skin just long enough to pull me close to their weight. My eyelids softened as the seconds passed. I kept them closed for fear of seeing the monster take shape in my room. But nothing moved in the bleak night except a constrained inhalation, followed by an involuntary exhalation, slowly, to not be heard—quietly, not to be noticed. I recognized the need to breathe.

A creak of the stairs awakened me in the space where night and morning blur. I poked my head out my door to see Dad sitting on the bottom stairs, lacing his work boots. Outside, the stars glistened dimly, so I knew it must be very early. Without a word, I tiptoed down the steps and hugged him from behind, kissing the scruff of his neck.

I whispered, "I love you."

"Be good," he replied.

Those words were as close as I ever came to receiving "I love you, too." I returned to bed, and as I drifted back to sleep, I wondered if I would ever be good enough for him to say it back.

Dad was close to me twice, of his own volition. I was sitting on his lap, watching television, my brown-frame glasses pressed into the bridge of my nose. A blue and gray flannel hat covered the top of my brown, stringy hair.

Each summer, Mom called us onto the front porch. With scissors in hand, she invited my sisters, Michelle and April, and me to take turns sitting on the yellow milk crate. Afterward, tumbleweeds of hair were swept from the porch. "For the birds to build nests," Mom added. Having two months before facing the ridicule of salon kids at school gave me time for my bangs to even out, if only long enough to pin them back. Hats and banana clips become as essential as swimsuits during those growing-out months.

I scratched the top of my head underneath the cap as Dad and I stared aimlessly at the screen before us. Most nights, he fell asleep, mouth agape, television blaring after dinner, and I stayed perched on his lap. On this rare occasion, Dad placed his large hand on my leg. I placed mine on top, detailing the calluses around each knuckle with the tip of my finger, grateful to feel the weight.

Another time, Dad hoisted me atop his broad shoulders. We stood like giants, six foot four, and I could finally see the world as he saw it, high above the rest. We watched Michelle and April perform over a sea of other parents sitting in cobalt blue plastic chairs on the side of a cinder block cafeteria. I had the best seat in the house.

The only thing I remember about the play is Dad holding me. The program ended, and he turned to Mom, "Laura, where's Christine?" She laughed, and he looked puzzled.

For a moment, there was silence. "Douglas, she's on your shoulders!"

"Oh," he said, lifting me slightly, only to let gravity drag my feet to the floor. Bodies obstructed my view as we exited the sterile cafeteria, his large hand leading me out the door. I did not know whether he knew he carried me on his shoulders the entire time.

One morning, I woke to sunshine blinding me through the vast panes of glass. I walked down the stairs to find Mom faithfully studying at the kitchen table. A thick ivory Bible was splayed open, pages outlined in gold. The book must have been very special because she kept it in an engraved wooden box when she wasn't reading from it. If you opened the tiny gold clasp, a very pale, wavy-haired Jesus gazed lovingly with light brown eyes. His arms were open as if to lift you into them and hold you close. I often stared back at him and wondered what it must feel like to be held that way.

The priest at our church read from the same book, but I never understood a word he said. I once raised my hand during Sunday School to ask about the holy water or the purpose of praying to Mary since she is dead.

None of the teachers had an answer but were quick to respond, "No more questions! Just listen."

When it was time for me to attend confession, each one of the students in our class stood in a neat line against the wall leading to the priest's office. I frantically scrolled through the list of wrongs the quiet critic in my mind replayed. How many times had I stolen one of Mom's homemade chocolate chip cookies from the jar? *There are probably too many to be forgiven.* What about that time I lied about . . . *well, certainly there is something I've lied about!* My feet shuffled nervously as I watched the solid black door open and shut as each classmate entered and exited, stepping to the back of the line when their session was finished. When it was my turn, I was ushered closer and instructed to wait outside. The rest of the class stood single-file behind me. I felt their eyes on my back. When the door cracked open, I held my breath, still unsure of which sin to divulge. Father Caffrey emerged from the room, his large white dress robe filled the expanse of the hallway.

"Come in," he smiled, waving a large hand toward the empty room.

I sat in the black leather chair across from a large mahogany desk. A picture of the Pope hung on the wall, and a smaller picture of the Virgin Mother Mary sat near the computer.

"Well," Father Caffrey began.

I folded my right foot over the left and placed my hands in my lap, clearing my throat. Be good.

With an audible exhalation, I blurted out, "I tried to commit suicide once."

Father Caffrey tilted his head to one side, and I wondered how the small white cap remained without tumbling to the ground.

"Go on," he spoke in a gentle and understanding manner.

"Well . . . ," I hesitated, "My Dad drinks a lot. Sometimes, he gets really angry. I guess I just didn't know what else to do. So, I climbed out of my room window and thought about what it would feel like to jump off."

"What did you do after you were on the roof?" he asked, still unphased by my shocking confession.

"I guess I realized there was still more to live for," I ended. I felt all of the wisdom of my seven-year-old words proudly.

Father Caffrey bowed his head and began to pray. My body grew warm as memories of Dad filled my mind.

Once again, I was lying in bed, peeking through my sheets. Dad was yelling at Michelle again. Michelle had locked herself in her room and threatened to jump out of her window.

I heard her scream, "What is the point of living when I have parents who treat me like a prisoner in my own home?"

Dad yelled back, reminding her this home does not belong to us children and that this is the house he built with his own hands. "As long as you live in *my* house," he continued, "you will follow *my* rules! In *my* house, you do not lock the doors!" Dad began to pound away at the wooden frame around her door, ripping it open.

I slipped underneath the comforter, squeezing Cinnamon Bear tightly. Mom appeared like an angel, blonde hair illuminated by the hallway's light. She stood between Dad and the shrapnel, but her tiny frame was unable to shield us all. The house and everyone in it received the wounds of his anger.

When Father Caffrey raised his head and unfolded his hands, I stared at him sullenly. "You are forgiven in the Name of the Father, in the Name of the Son, and in the Name of the Holy Ghost," he said, dipping his finger into a small dish, extending his thumb, and marking a cross on my forehead. When I stand to leave, I am acutely aware that lying to a priest is a sin. Finally, I have something to confess, but it is too late. I am already standing in the hallway with the rest of the oily sinners.

Maggie was my only friend at church. A four-wheeler trail meandered through the woods from the back of our neighborhood to her house. When the path cleared, two lakes emerged beside a tan-colored brick mansion. Maggie's dad let my dad fish there, even though her dad was never home. Dad and I drove the four-wheeler to the lake often during the summer. We stood side-by-side on the lake's edge, dangling the writhing worms into the muddy water. Dad helped me unhook the sunfish and perch I caught, which he said were just for throwing back in the lake. He showed me how to wiggle their tails gently back and forth before setting them free, giving them momentum to catch their breath underneath the water. Sometimes, when I lie back in the bathtub, I think about those fish and see how long I can hold my breath under the water before coming up for air.

Maggie had two pet ducks, Bubbles and Bruiser, that lived around the lake. The closest my sisters and I ever got to having our own pets was when April brought home something wounded from the yard. The random array of flightless birds, terrified cats, or the occasional baby opossum survived a few days on the back porch before I had to search through the basement for an empty shoebox to administer a proper burial. Maggie's older brother was in the same grade as April. I always wondered if they thought about being boyfriend and girlfriend or if it was too weird since we lived in a pet cemetery in a log cabin through the woods.

Their house sat a quarter mile off the main road, the driveway winding through a field of hay bales with no horses in sight. For a moment, I imagined spinning in circles through the fields, singing like Belle from *Beauty and the Beast*. As we got closer, the balconies emerged on each side of the awning. I waited to see if the Beast would appear in the window. A spiral staircase wound upward through the French doors, separating opposite sides of the upper-level hallways toward the bedrooms. Maggie and I raced up either side to see who could reach her room the fastest. Her house had five bedrooms and bathrooms, so no one shared a room like April and me in our bunk beds.

Maggie's dad drove an old tan Jeep with no doors or windows. When I asked Maggie why her dad had so much money but drove a car like that, Maggie laughed. She led me down the stairs to the garage. The space was bare except for a large tarp draped over the shape of a vehicle. Maggie lifted the edge open to expose the frame of a powder blue car. As I ran my finger over the jaguar affixed on the front hood, flecks of silver shimmered throughout the side.

"He never drives it," Maggie said in a matter-of-fact tone. "My brother said when he gets old enough, he's going to fix it and drive it himself."

"Is it broken?" I asked, still in awe.

Maggie shrugged her shoulders and tugged on the rest of the plastic covering, revealing the convertible top and creamy leather seats. My mind flashed to the old James Bond films Dad would leave on the television while he slept in the recliner. An attractive woman with oversized sunglasses and a handkerchief holding back her windblown hair laughed in the passenger seat. "Have you ever ridden in it?" I continued as if in a daydream of Hollywood wonder.

"We used to when we still lived in Michigan," Maggie replied, "but not since we moved to Georgia. I was just a baby when we moved, so I don't really remember."

Maggie led me to the library, opening another set of heavy French doors. Cherry wood shelves lined each wall with books of every color, neatly coordinated in rows. I twirled around the velvet-lined couch and coffee table that looked like they had never been used.

"Tale as old as time . . . " I begin to sing[1]

Maggie stopped me midline, placing her finger over her lips. "What?" I asked.

"We're not supposed to be in here," she said quietly, grabbing my hand and walking me over to a tiny square piece of wood between the shelves. Eyes wide, Maggie unlatched a hidden shelf behind the bookcase. Intricate glass bottles filled with brown liquid sat neatly in a circle.

"I'm not supposed to know about these," she whispered.

I was too embarrassed to ask because I didn't know what the bottles were or what they contained. Shrugging my shoulders, I whispered, "I won't tell anyone."

We laughed quietly, sharing a secret between us to seal our friendship. I felt proud to hold the weight.

"Want a snack?" Maggie asked, and we skipped out of the Beast's forbidden west wing into the kitchen.

A water fountain separated the stove from the food pantry, which was filled almost as high as the stacks of books in the library. Maggie's mom made popcorn for us in a giant dome container that resembled an alien spaceship. She sprayed the kernels with a butter alternative I had never seen. Maggie's mom was a plain woman with short, curly hair and wide-framed glasses that covered most of her face. Her brown pleated pants accentuated the boxiness of her form. As she stood over the popcorn bowl, I tried to imagine her riding alongside Maggie's tall, handsome father in his James Bond car.

Maggie opened a humungous built-in refrigerator that matched the rest of the cabinets, similar to the hidden door inside the library. She popped open a silver lid from a tall aluminum can and offered me a taste. I scrunched my nose and asked why she had weight-loss drinks.

"It's good and will make you stay skinny," Maggie responded simply. I grabbed the can from her and took a gulp. It was thick and chalky. I licked the sweet chocolate flavor from my lips and smiled. We were not allowed to have sugar in our house, so even if I didn't need a weight-loss drink, it still tasted like a treat.

On the desk in the living room was a tiny yellowish computer. Maggie pressed a button on the screen to show me how to play the Wheel of Fortune game. Vanna White appeared with her flowing dress. I pushed the arrow key to see her walk and turned over the green cube to reveal an answer to the question at the bottom of the screen.

"If I don't get famous singing or as an actress, maybe I can be a game show host like Vanna," I told Maggie, eyes transfixed on the tall, skinny blonde figure walking slowly back and forth on the screen.

"We can go upstairs to play dress up if you want," Maggie suggested.

Maggie's bedroom was the size of our living room; a sizable sweeping canopy hung from the tall posters on her bed. Two private balconies overlooked the koi pond in front of the house. Her vanity sat between two closets filled with dress-up clothes and jewelry. Movie star light bulbs outlined the exterior of the mirror. Maggie and I picked out feather boas and brightly colored leotards for our song and dance performance. I had never worn makeup before, so Maggie taught me to sweep the rose-colored blush in circles on my cheeks before applying blue eye shadow upward until it hit my eyebrows. She smeared on dark pink lipstick and pressed her lips together to form a kiss in the mirror. We danced around the room, singing at the top of our lungs, spinning in circles until dizzy.

When it was time for bed, I gathered Cinnamon Bear and jumped into the tall bed fit for a princess. Maggie rolled over onto her pink satin pillowcase she called "silky" and whispered, "Do you want to play pretend with our pillows?"

"What do you mean?" I asked, confused.

"You get on top of your pillow like this." Maggie placed the pillow underneath herself and began smacking noises, her face planted deep inside the fabric.

"This is how you kiss a boy," she laughed.

"How do you know how to kiss a boy?" I replied.

She looked up from "silky" and said, "You just learn."

I had seen my parents kiss on very few occasions. My romance education mostly surfaced from the final scene of *Beauty and the Beast* when the Beast transformed into a different-looking man. In a swarm of magic, Belle and the Prince dramatically embrace and kiss one another.

Leaving my imagination, I asked, "But how did you learn?"

Maggie paused for a moment, considering.

"Pretend you're a baby," she continued, "and your dad is asleep. You go to get in bed with him, and he accidentally has sex with you."

Maggie began kissing her pillow, but this time, she was writhing around in the sheets. Unsure of what sex meant, I stopped and observed. I kicked my legs a few times and made a few noises. After a minute, I rolled over to my side, facing away, "I'm tired. Goodnight."

Squeezing Cinnamon Bear, I lay still, hoping she thought I was asleep.

When Maggie's mom called to invite me over the following Friday, I declined the offer. I decided to see if Natalie and Amanda could play. In the morning, I walked down the street to the neighbor's house, where their mother, Darlene, greeted me with a large milk jug. The bright yellow container matched the pat of butter melting down the mountain of piping hot grits sitting on the counter.

"Would you like some breakfast?" Darlene smiled.

As we sat around the dining room table, Amanda declared that she was legally changing her name to include both of my sisters, proudly explaining, "My whole name is now Amanda April Michelle Williams."

Everyone laughed, but she never backed down from it being the truth. I wondered how switching my middle name from Diane to Natalie would work. Christine Natalie Warhola. Natalie felt like a big sister most days. My sister, Michelle, is seven years older than me, and my sister, April, is only two years behind her. They spent a lot of time away from the house with their friends. Over the next few months, I became a weekend staple at Natalie and Amanda's house, welcomed by the smell of bacon and grits. The Williams' house became my home away from home, a sanctuary of sisterhood.

Summer heat dampened our beds, and Natalie, Amanda, and I conspired to spend our weeknights camping. Their dad, Tim, built trails behind his house that led to a campsite surrounded by large pines. Four logs marked the clearing where a meager fire pit nestled in the middle, surrounded by large gray stones. To us, it was the symbol of freedom, the altar of s'more heaven. We unfolded the tent's flaps, and I learned to stake each one down with a long metal rod, pressing deeply into the earth to keep it in place. Then, we took turns hoisting up the sides of the tent to admire our temporary home. On the occasion that Trevor and his dad joined us, Trevor slept outside in a sleeping bag by the fire. Amanda and I whispered low in the tent as the stars sprayed across the canopy. We giggled over the prospect that one of us could marry Trevor when we grew up. After days of riding bikes and running through sprinklers, Trevor and I played with Barbies together. It was a kindness he extended to me. I think of it often.

At Trevor's birthday party, Amanda told me she would try to kiss him. I scrunched my nose in disgust at the thought of Maggie flailing around in bed.

"I'm pretty sure you will get in trouble if you do that. I think you're only supposed to kiss the boy you will marry," I replied.

Amanda looked at me, her large lips curling upward. She laughed.

Eyes wide, she said plainly, "I've gotten so many whippins'! What's one more? Anyway, one of us will marry Trevor, so I may as well kiss him first!"

Amanda's mischievous grin remained as she skipped past the arcade games, her long blonde ponytail swishing back and forth. I overheard Trevor's mom telling my mom that Trevor snuck out of the house with his dad's pocket knife and carved T + C into the trunk of an old tree. His dad had discovered it while looking for firewood.

My mom responded, "Oh brother!" with hands on her hips, lips pressed tightly. I am reassured of her disapproval, knowing I didn't need to feel the pressure of learning to kiss a boy! And yet, it felt special to have someone carve part of my name into something permanent. Trevor blew out the candles, and I took a big bite of cake, resolving never to mention the carvings for fear he would stop playing with me.

Chapter 2

When the new school year began, an influx of unfamiliar faces charged into the fourth-grade classrooms. A number of boys were as cute as Trevor, and Amanda finally gave up the belief that one of us had to marry him. As we walked from the school bus down the street, Amanda invited me to her house to play with baby dolls. She pretended she was a mom, sticking an assortment of pillows or plastic dolls up her shirt. We laughed as Amanda begged her mom to have another baby. Natalie, who is two years older, was beginning middle school. I waited until she came home to sneak away to talk about boys. As Natalie and I huddled underneath the down comforter of her bed, she asked me who I had a crush on. I confessed that a boy once kissed me on the cheek behind the playground. My face turned hot with embarrassment as I shared my fear of Mom finding out and getting angry with me. Natalie assured me that my secret was safe with her, and I was at ease knowing she was someone I could trust. She shared about going to football games and mingling with cheerleaders. Natalie confided in me that she had never kissed a boy, but she told me about all the other girls in her class who had. We both giggled with unknowing excitement.

While the weather was warm, we continued to sleep outside at our campsite. Natalie and Amanda's dad and mine took turns seeing who could eat the hottest chili peppers from the garden. Tim's naturally rosy cheeks blazed as he pulled a flask of apple cider vinegar from his pocket to wash the scorching burn from his lips. He followed the vinegar with another shot of beer. Natalie and Amanda made jokes with their dad, laughing and hugging him. Tim told us stories and recounted days of working as a garbage man, as a volunteer fireman, and in the army. He placed a marshmallow on a stick and handed it to me. I wrapped my arms around his neck and hugged him as if his arms could somehow be an extension of my Dad's arms. I thought about the picture of Jesus inside the box and was comforted.

Every few months, our two families would scrounge enough money to eat at a tiny Mexican restaurant in the adjacent town. Natalie, Amanda, and I ordered large bowls of white cheese dip and waited until our dads had a few drinks to steal a quarter or two from their pockets. Mom was strict about our sugar consumption and only allowed foods in the house to contain six grams or less. On these rare occasions, I pressed the silver coin in my hand and stood before the candy machines for minutes before solidifying a decision. Natalie and I took turns shaking the machine for one another as we turned the cold, silver dial, hoping that just a few more pieces of candy would dislodge from their home. The red, cinnamon-flavored pellets poured into my hand, and I savored each individually. After a few hours of loud joking and Tim using a poor blend of Spanish and English words with the waiters, he threw his shoe into the kitchen to incite some attention. The wait staff came out either cheering or scolding, and we waited to see how much time was left before we were asked to leave.

Natalie, Amanda, and I squeezed into the backseat of Tim's beat-up red truck. Windows down, we sang country music as loud as our voices could carry into the night sky. Tim slowed the vehicle to a stop in the middle of a windy road.

"Get out," he gently commanded, head sticking out the window. "Look at all them stars. Man, them are some pretty lights up there! Come on, get out!"

Tim pushed the creaking door open and stepped onto the pavement. There were no other lights for miles around. An open field was on the right, dotted with a few cows, and a tall forest of pines on our left. I was still balancing one foot on a yellow rectangle in the road. We stared silently at the vast array of stars piercing through the darkness. I wanted to pluck them from the sky and place the light inside my chest, to have something or someone illuminate who I was inside. *God*, I thought to myself as a silent prayer. *You must be good.* I felt small in the open space, under the grandeur of the night sky. The story of the sky felt bigger than my ability to rationalize my humanity or the thought of God. I breathed in the crisp air and felt peace in the exhale. After a while of silent wonder, we piled back into the vehicle. Tim drove down the road with his door ajar, his leg extended like a bicycle joyride. Our sides cramped as we doubled over from laughter and too much cheese dip.

On weekends, when Mom was not teaching step aerobics at the racquetball center, we drove to strangers' houses, which she cleaned while I watched television. I scrambled into the station wagon, caught between the oil soap and an old gray vacuum cleaner. At 11 o'clock, I sat cross-legged in front of a screen and waited anxiously as the camera panned the audience, looking for the next person to be called down to spin a gigantic wheel. The girls on the show were beautiful. *I want to be beautiful one day*, I thought to myself. There was only one woman I had ever seen in that town who looked like the girls on television. After Mom had finished cleaning and received her check, we drove into town to deposit the money. A bank teller waved to us from the glass inside the building. She had the longest hair I had ever seen, bangs standing tall above her forehead. She wore pink lipstick so bright I could see the color from the car window. Mom drove through the columns that held the transparent rockets and shot the check through a tube in the ceiling. I waited to hear the *swoosh* sound it made when the money was sucked up and delivered. The beautiful woman sent a lollipop for me back with the deposit slip. None of the flavors of lollipops tasted like the fruit they were masquerading, but I ate it anyway. I looked over at Mom. She was beautiful, too, but not in the same way as the bank lady. Mom was petite and blonde with blue eyes and thin lips. I wondered how it felt for her to have blonde hair and blue eyes when all three of her daughters have brown hair and brown eyes. I wonder if Mom ever thought about wearing lipstick.

After years of piecing together work, Mom applied to be a teacher's assistant at my elementary school. We got in the car together again for work but in a new environment this time. I was grateful I no longer had to ride the school bus. Ms. Debbie asked Mom if I would like to sing outside the classroom at her church.

"I've been listening to her sing when she does her work and during recess. Christine has a beautiful voice, and I think the congregation would love it."

When we got into the car to leave school, I waited for Mom's response. I feared she would know I was eavesdropping if I brought it up. Mom never mentioned the conversation. I assumed Ms. Debbie didn't realize we were Catholic. Maybe it was inappropriate for me to go on stage at a different kind of church. My hopes to build on my future singing career had been halted. I sat silently for the rest of the car ride home, trying to hide my tears.

Excitement was reignited when Mom began preparations for the annual neighborhood picnic. My world contained nine houses, each with a family as dysfunctional as my own. We were all messy and utterly average from where I stood. Our neighbors were our family. After decorating handwritten invitations, I excitedly strolled down the street, carefully placing a card inside each metal mailbox. The neighborhood kids began chatting, formulating ideas for what they would perform at the talent show. The week leading up to the picnic, Natalie, Amanda, and Trevor weaved in and out of the basement, practicing their parts for the play or rehearsing dance steps. I spent my evenings alone in my room, listening to the song from my dad's collection of country music that I chose to perform.

Our neighbors gathered on the front lawn on the picnic day, setting up chairs and swimming in our above-ground pool. As smoke rose from the grill, Dad revealed his toothy grin as he proudly displayed whatever animal he had killed. Mom decorated the table with a salad, adding some greenery to the neutral casseroles and potato salad display. With the dampening humidity just beginning to settle in, the shallow pool was a reprieve. We swam until it was time to eat together. A feast was laid on checkered red and white plastic with mismatched folding tables scattered across the driveway.

With the clearing of paper plates and darkness enfolding the lawn, the adults made their way to the lawn chairs while the kids gathered on the makeshift stage. Chest held high, I stepped onto the grandstand that was our front porch. I had changed out of my bathing suit into jeans and a flannel shirt. Dad's cowboy hat perched on top of my long brown hair. Dad had a picture of Reba McEntire in the garage next to his assortment of tools and deer antlers. She was dazzling in her red dress and wild hair. I channeled her wide mouth and belted out the next few lines with gusto. When I hit the last note, my sister April pressed STOP on the boombox connected to a bright orange extension cord. There was a pause before everyone cheered. I took a deeply dramatic bow, and a smile lifted onto my flushed cheeks. *Who needs a church stage to sing when you have a yard filled with neighbors at your own front door?*

When the moon was high and cicadas joined the welcoming song of summer, neighbors reluctantly folded their chairs. They took their time hugging their goodbyes as though they'd traveled farther than a few houses down the street. Bellies filled and lungs sharp from running, swimming, and singing. Rest came quickly.

Provision came in the form of venison on the table. Dad and Tim came home from hunting excursions, calling for my sisters and me to meet him in the driveway. Without warning, Dad jumped in the truck bed and raised up the limp head by the antlers, grinning widely. Michelle rolled her eyes and walked back into the house without a word while April moved closer to examine the latest kill. I never understood what made her so curious about dead or near-dead animals. After standing in the driveway for a minute or two longer, I followed Michelle inside and tried to shake the image from my mind.

When my sisters invited friends to the house for dinner, Dad claimed we were eating opossums. Sticking the end of the fork in his ear, he burped loudly. After a while, my sisters stopped inviting people to eat with us or dinner with us altogether. Mom attempted to smooth things over by reciting a prayer. The words ran together in a monotonous trail. I tried to mumble along or keep my eyes closed until it was over. When Dad was in good spirits, he would hijack the prayer with his own benediction, "Rub a dub dub, thanks for the grub. Yay, God." Michelle rolled her eyes, and April pinned me with a threatening look to preempt my laughter that would show approval for Dad's behavior. I shrugged my shoulders and half-grinned to let her know I thought it was slightly humorous but thoroughly disrespectful. Mom responded in her typical fashion, nudging Dad and saying, "Dear," which I interpreted as "deer." I couldn't determine why the sentimental language in marriage pertained to the same animal we ate for dinner.

Sharpsburg was so quiet you could hear people before you saw them. The hum of an engine interrupted our feast of venison and potatoes. As Tim pulled into the gravel drive, Dad looked up from the table through the window in the living room and stood to meet him outside. A few minutes later, from below us, there was a commotion. Mom and April looked at one another and rushed down the basement stairs.

"Oh my gosh!" Mom exclaimed from below, and April began to laugh.

Michelle and I dropped our forks and slowly rose from our chairs. Tim and Dad had a large deer cornered inside a makeshift barricade, and April was gathering more folding tables to secure the surrounding area. The deer looked frightened, legs buckling beneath him with each frantic step. Finally, Mom threw a bundle of blankets into the pen's center, and the confused animal lay down in its newly discovered home.

April scavenged for a shallow bowl of water. After the noise settled, we all walked upstairs.

Tim sat down and explained, "Your dad here's been boastin' all huntin' season 'bout shootin' them deer. I hadn't got a single one, so I was drivin' down Doc Fischer road when I seen this deer that'd just been hit by a car. I thought I'd bring it by here and tell ya'll I'd shot it myself seein' how big it is. I done got halfway down the street when I looked in the mirror and seen that thing standin' up in the back of the truck! Scared me half to death. Must've been stunned and not dead, I reckon. But it's still hurt. Probably be back up and healthy in a day or so."

Tim finished, but Dad was laughing so hard he was on the floor. We joined in with a burst of anxious, bellowing laughter.

Wiping tears, Dad finally said, "Well, what d'ya want me to do with it?"

Tim grinned, "He'll be fine. Just let 'im rest, and you can let 'im out of the basement or add 'im to your antler collection."

April was beside herself with excitement. "I'll take care of him, Daddy!" she committed.

"Welp, I guess we'll see what happens," Dad agreed. I began wondering if there were boxes big enough to bury the deer's body once it died.

Each day after school that week, I opened the basement door slowly and walked down the steep staircase to see our new pet. The giant animal attempted to stand but slumped down against the concrete floor, its black eyes wide and maddening. By the end of the week, I walked down the stairs to find the young buck was gone. When I asked Mom about it, she said Dad let it go back into the wild. As we sat around the dinner table that night, all I could envision were those two dark eyes as I chewed the venison slowly. Michelle looked down at her plate and declared she was a vegetarian.

Michelle was rarely home once her friends began to drive. When she was away, I would sneak into her bedroom to rattle through her drawers, pulling a CD from its jacket. A departure from the country music Dad listened to in his truck, Michelle's music blared electric guitars with angst-filled female voices. I was enamored. I picked out an oversized blue t-shirt with a swirl design, cinching it with a rubber band to my waist. Staring at myself in the mirror, I lip-synced the lyrics until I knew them by heart. Behind a large painted chest, drawings of names and flowers cascaded to the floorboards. I heard her come in at night when I was already in my bed, the creak of the stairs leading up to her bedroom. She and Mom exchanged hurried words in whispers before Mom disappeared into her room. A gentle snoring reverberated through the cracks in the beams. I pretended to be asleep as Michelle slipped out the door and into another car waiting in the driveway.

Thick calluses formed on my feet as I walked down the gravel away from our log cabin. The trail extended into a forest of tall pines adjacent to the cornfield across the street, leading to Mr. Murphy's house. Murphy had a tuft of white hair that lifted brightly against his darkened skin. I watched from the driveway as he rode his tractor across the field of corn stalks, their golden arms fanning in the summer heat. Dad told me Murphy knew much about the land because he was mostly Cherokee. Perched atop his tractor, Murphy lifted his arm and waved to me, mimicking the movement of the corn. He was a man of few words, and the ones he spoke came out muffled. From what I could tell, it was because he was Native American, and I had difficulty understanding his native tongue. It wasn't until I began middle school that Murphy's liver began to fail. I realized alcohol was more than likely a factor in his garbled tongue.

Dad took me over to Murphy's house on occasion. Murphy's wife, Maddie, was in the kitchen to greet us, stirring up the beginnings of a casserole with another can of creamed vegetable soup. The air was thick with grease and smoke when we entered. The walls were a faded yellow, reminding me of my bedroom. I was relieved to finally go downstairs, where the pool table stood like an altar in the center of the darkened basement. Whenever Dad played pool, he laughed a lot. It made me feel proud to sit with those men. Cigarette smoke filled the tiny room while pool balls clacked against the sides of one another. Dad laughed more when he drank. He also yelled more.

When Dad and Michelle's yelling escalated, I ran away. Cutting across the dirt path worn down by four-wheeler tracks, I paused to consider how long it would take my parents to find me. I walked until no one was in sight and squatted down to hide. I waited seven minutes before thinking my parents had forgotten entirely I existed, and tears formed as I thought it was likely the case. Waiting another three minutes, I turned toward home, wondering what Mom was making for dinner.

The first time Michelle ran away, it lasted more than the ten minutes I mustered up that day in the woods. Mom called all the neighbors, and Dad took off on his four-wheeler. Just before the sunset, Dad returned with Michelle riding on the back of the four-wheeler. No one spoke that night.

A few nights later, Michelle picked me up from a friend's house, and we took a detour to the grocery store. "I just need to grab something really quickly," she said, letting go of my hand.

"Why don't you go down the next aisle, and I will meet you."

I nodded and turned around. I turned back toward her, unsure if she meant the aisle to my left or right. Michelle took a bottle from the shelf and placed it underneath her baggy t-shirt. Confused, I walked toward her quickly.

"What are you doing?" I asked.

"Shhh. Nothing," She grabbed my hands and twirled me around the aisle. My mind spun with me as I reached into my coat pocket to reveal a crisp twenty-dollar bill Mom had given me.

"Look! I have money," I announced triumphantly.

Michelle's hand swiped the air, shoving the money back into my pocket. Her hand tightened around mine as we increased pace and walked straight for the doors. As we breezed past the cash registers, the doors made a clean *swish* as we walked into the night. My heart was racing, and I could barely open my mouth when Michelle gasped and pointed, "Look! It's snowing!"

My breath weighed heavily against the guilt and the cold. Wisps of air drifted from my mouth, but I could not speak. I watched as the miracle of Georgia snow swayed down from the darkness above. I was a solitary drifter, uniquely shaped for beautiful grief. As we stepped inside Michelle's car, I turned toward the window, pretending to watch the flakes dance. Instead, I hid my tears, feeling the knot twist in my stomach as we approached home. I walked silently into the house, up the stairs to my room, and cried myself to sleep.

I grabbed an oversized green corduroy coat and draped it around my petite frame. Having two older sisters, their shared clothes became my hand-me-downs. Mom and I stared out the windshield as we drove down the familiar strip of road that led from our neighborhood past the long row of trailers. Toilets were used as flower pots in one yard, and tattered flags drooped next to the pile of cars with no wheels. Before we made it to the town square to run errands, we passed by the grocery store where Michelle and I had been just days before. I glanced at Mom, trying to observe any expression that would let me know if she knew I was an unwilling accomplice to theft. When she continued driving, eyes fixed, I sighed in relief. Reaching my hand into my pocket, I felt the outline of the twenty-dollar bill in my imagination. Instead, I pulled out a small plastic bag filled with dried green leaves. Mom looked in my direction.

"What's that?" Mom asked.

I shrugged my shoulders. "It's Michelle's coat," I said, still holding the bag before my face.

Mom slowed the car to a stop, her eyes tired. She removed the bag from my hand and placed it in the console, out of sight. She turned the car around without a word and drove us back home. Our home thundered quietly with discord. There were late-night calls and hushed conversations about bonds and jail. In the weeks to come, I would begin to understand that silence was its own form of communication, passed down from generation to generation.

Midway through the school year, the English teacher pulled me aside in the hallway.

"There is a new girl at our school," she told me. "Her name is Britney. I want you to show her around and make her feel welcome. She'll be coming into the classroom any minute."

"Ok, I can do that!" I responded, enjoying the extra attention.

Britney's long blonde hair cascaded down her cream-colored turtleneck. She had a slender waist and a new pair of denim jeans with jewels on the pockets. Her shimmery lip gloss matched the pale hue of pink on her nails. I looked down at my hand-me-down pants and oversized t-shirt from my sister's closet, combing my fingers through the ends of my hair. Britney looked up at me. Her eyes were shaped like the wild deer in our basement, and I could see her fear.

In a low tone, she said, "Hi."

As I began to describe the teachers and different kids in the class who were my friends, she smiled. "Thank you," she said.

I was enamored as I watched her shiny lips form each word.

In a town of 324 people, being recognized as an outsider was easy. It was only a few days before every boy in school talked about how pretty Britney was, and every girl was writing notes behind her back. Since I had the job of befriending her, I basked in the glow of her newfound popularity. When I found out she lived in the neighborhood that had recently been built within walking distance from my home, I knew I needed to find a way to be close to her. In the afternoon, I stepped onto the bus to see Britney seated in the back with the older kids. She was alone, so I asked to sit with her. I was a moth to her light. Our bus driver flipped the radio station on as the bus filled and the engine turned. Britney and I looked at one another and began singing along. Laughter broke the tension of our new friendship. We sang the rest of the way home.

After a few months, I convinced Mom to let me ride the bus to her house. Most days, Britney's mom and dad were not home until after dinner, but I left that detail out. We dropped our backpacks by the door, and Britney told her younger sister to play outside.

"My soap is on," Britney announced, sitting on the couch and turning on the television.

"Your what?" I asked.

"My soap . . . you know, soap opera," she clarified.

"I don't know what that means," I confessed. "Mom doesn't like me watching television, and my dad usually watches sports if anything is on."

"You're going to love it." Britney began to fill me in on the plot, detailing steamy love stories and which characters are evil.

"Our television only gets five channels most days," I laughed nervously.

"That's lame," Britney said nonchalantly. "I guess you'll just have to come over here more."

I sighed, relieved that she still wanted to be friends. The girls in our class had begun to form groups and sign contracts about who could hang out together. As Britney continued being invited into more cliques, part of me wondered how much room would be left for me. After a couple of weeks of watching shows and looking at the teen magazines Britney's mom purchased for her, Britney began initiating truth-or-dare scenarios. The games led to the same end as the ones played by Maggie—kissing and touching. Saying no because of my discomfort only jeopardized my ability to be friends with her. Britney's popularity had escalated since she started attending our school, and I was only slightly noticed based on proximity. Instead of distancing myself as I had done with Maggie, I complied with her every demand.

While spending the night, Britney became increasingly frustrated by my unwillingness to choose "dare" in the game *Truth or Dare*. She changed the game to *dare* or *dare*, and after trying to fight my way out, she told me I had to treat Cinnamon Bear like my boyfriend. Britney gave specific instructions when I confessed I didn't know what that meant. Feeling uncomfortable but too scared of losing the best friend I had, I followed her every word. A flash of heat came over my body. I thought of Maggie and the people on the television shows, and a seed of shame was planted. The weight of missing the mark in my genuine desire to say "no" fell heavy on my chest. I had become flawed, and now I had no priest to confess my sin.

The more time Britney and I spent together, the more curious and, consequently, more anxious I became. I began riding the bus again in the afternoons to get home before Mom, racing to turn on the television and watch Britney's "soap." I stared at the screen, waiting to see if someone would kiss or remove their clothes to get underneath the sheets together. I waited to feel the new sensations that had awakened. Still, it was a mystery what this truly meant. I had only ever seen my parents kiss on special occasions, and it seemed as obligatory as saying thank you for a gift you didn't really like. My parents had never spoken to me about sex. The few times I heard the word was by an older kid on the school bus. When the older kid made a vulgar gesture, I felt sick. When I asked my mom what he meant, she casually told me to ignore him. Watching this passionate interaction between strangers ignited an intense curiosity about how it could feel so different. I sat, transfixed to the television, my finger poised on the "back" button to quickly change the channel in case Mom came home early from work.

The desire to connect with a human in a way where lips touch, hands collide, promises are made, and lives become inseparable consumed me. Pages of diary entries detailed names and dreams of boys that a part of my subconscious heart wanted someone to fill. Desire shifted from being a young child who longed to be held to gaining the attention of any boy within reach. Confused and ashamed, I restlessly awakened my sexuality behind closed doors. *Touch me. Hug Me. Tell me I belong. That I am valuable. That I am worth something. Tell me I am lovable.*

Chapter 3

The transition from elementary to middle school, complete with hormones and tears, was punctuated by my decision to stop attending Catholic church. Mom allowed me to begin attending a non-denominational church on Wednesday nights with a new friend from school named Anna. The sanctuary was filled with very normal-looking people who did not talk about bathing in holy water or praying to dead people. They bathed in well or city water and prayed to Jesus, who they claimed was alive, although He died once. I liked what I heard about a loving Father who wanted to be close to me and forgive me for the bad things I had done, making my life better. Groups of kids our age gathered together to learn songs, read the Bible, play games, and eat pizza.

Anna's family was warm and welcoming. They laughed, played music together, watched movies, and conversed in the kitchen while sipping from large soda cups. Anna had the longest hair I had ever seen, cascading down her back to her waist. Her large blue eyes lit up as we blared music in her room and sang along. Anna's older sister was the same age as my sister, April, and even had the same name! April sat on top of Anna's bed at night and told us what it was like to have a boyfriend. I asked a million questions. April told us what it felt like to kiss boys and listen to them serenade her with love songs they would play on the guitar. It sounded so romantic, not like how Maggie or Britney depicted it or the soap operas. I reveled in April's stories, curious if my sister had had the same experiences. Anna and I giggled as April dramatically recalled the details of her evenings, telling us that one day, we would have boyfriends, too. Anna insisted she was not interested in any of the boys at our school. She maintained a quiet confidence that lacked nothing. On the other hand, I listed three or four boys I thought were cute. Anna rolled her eyes and laughed, "You sound boy crazy!" We laughed until our sides hurt, mimicking April's stories and wondering what it would be like to be in high school one day.

My sister, April, was a ghost in our house. She drifted in and out, making noise when she needed attention, and then would leave again without a trace. She was distant, bossy, and brilliant. Occasionally, I found her playing the piano or painting, displaying talents I could only dream of possessing. Her test scores and athletic skills outweighed my own, and she exuded confidence. April was able to share some of the hobbies Dad would never be able to share with a boy child. Dad occasionally took her hunting and fishing with him and attended every softball game she played. I wondered if April felt more like the son Dad never had. I wondered if he ever told her he loved her.

When a boy in my Literature class approached me in the hallway, I quickly said yes to being his girlfriend. We sat together in the cafeteria and wrote poetry, sneaking notes during class and reciting Shakespeare. When invited to my first party outside of school, I snuck into April's closet and found a pair of wide-legged pants and a v-neck shirt. I let Anna fix my hair and apply shimmery lip gloss. There was mistletoe hanging from a beam in the barn where we danced. When Daniel kissed me, I felt it all the way to my toes. It was electric, and I smiled until my face hurt the following day. I was in love.

Daniel sat in the row behind me during band class, claiming my attention by making kissing noises. My girlfriends and I giggled down the row as we prepared ourselves for the next clarinet piece. I narrowed my eyes at him, not wanting to get into trouble with the teacher. He passed me a note folded in the shape of an obscure animal. I opened it discreetly to find an intricately detailed drawing of two hands and the words written above it: *I love you*. My heart dripped, and I fantasized about his lips on mine again.

To my surprise, Dad and Mom began attending church

with me. The pastor was preaching about how Jesus wanted to take away our sins. Like fire, he wants to refine us and make our hearts pure. "Only Jesus can do that!" The pastor bellowed enthusiastically from the stage. Then, his voice got quiet, "Somebody here, today, needs to know Jesus loves them. If that person is you, you must stand up and walk down the aisle. Let Jesus know you want to be saved from your sins!" The piano began to play softly, and at first, no one moved. A woman a few rows behind me began to take light gasps and sniffles. I noticed tears were soaking the front of my own shirt. I was blocked in the row by both my Mom and Dad. I stood up and shuffled through their legs. As I approached the front of the stage, I noticed a few other people were already praying. I knelt down. My forehead pressed against the rough carpet, and I began to weep uncontrollably. *I don't know what this means, but I want to know I am loved.*

When I told the Sunday School teacher I had already been baptized as a baby, she smiled, "That's ok, honey. That was not your decision. You've accepted Jesus in your heart to be your Lord and Savior. Now, you get to let everyone in the church know you have decided to follow Jesus!"

Mom and Dad chose to join me. We went to a class together where the church leaders told us what it meant to be saved. The teacher reminded us we were to live now "pure and blameless," and I immediately felt the guilt of all of the time I spent watching soap operas, the secret games with friends, and the cookies I had definitely stolen. Mostly, I felt guilty for having any feelings at all. Perfection felt out of reach, and I almost gave up altogether. Instead, I clenched my fist into a grip of perfect obedience. If following the rules was all it took to be loved, I was ready to be first in line . . . I mean, last in line. The teacher gave recommendations on what to wear during our baptisms when I became increasingly aware of two things outside my control. The first was that my legs had begun to grow dark hair, and shorts were now embarrassing in a room filled with neatly shaven girls my age. The second was that I had started to form breasts that could not be hidden in a wet t-shirt, and I did not want to cause any boys to lust.

I asked Mom if I could begin shaving early, which she

agreed was reasonable with the caveat, "You know that once you start shaving, you must keep doing it. You really should just wait as long as possible." Mom held a list of rules to transition into middle school normality: age 13 - clear lip gloss, age 14 - color lip gloss, age 15 - mascara, age 16 - ear piercing. I counted shaving early as an appropriate deviation from the rules and chose the baggiest t-shirt in my drawer to set out for our baptism day.

The morning Mom, Dad, and I were baptized, we each said a few words to a large crowd of people, got dunked, and came out of the water to a chorus of cheering. There was nothing magical about the water, but I felt clean. I told Jesus I would not watch TV with people underneath sheets, I would stop listening to songs with cuss words, and I would try to fall asleep at night without touching myself. I prayed that the waters of baptism would cure my sexuality, but I wanted to keep kissing Daniel.

By the age of thirteen, I learned what it meant to *maintain*. The tension of ongoing arguments between my sisters and Dad left my prayers to dust. I escaped in the sensations of my skin, mountains of books, and writing. Placing the pen to the paper, outcries of poetic verse leaped from the page. I leaned into the feeling writing gave me, asking teachers to lend me books and drowning myself in any poetry I could comprehend. Written words gave me a voice within the silence. It was solace and an escape amidst the claps of thunder reverberating as angry outbursts in our home. As the tension rumbled, I immediately fled to my bedroom. Dad began drinking heavily again as yelling pervaded the slats between the wooden planks. When the sound became unbearable, I wrapped myself heavily in sheets and found places on my body that pleasure could mask. I bore the pain of longing in my skin. In the darkness of my room, I fell asleep after the anxieties passed, crying for the shame of being born into a family that was too loud to listen to and too distracted to see me.

The next time Michelle disappeared, six months passed before we heard from her. My childhood prayers had always been songs that welled up from inside while cleaning windows, barefoot dancing in the front yard, and thank you's as the warmth of blankets lulled me to sleep. The Holy Spirit was present before It had a name. Now that I was attending a church, we were taught to talk to God as if "He" were our friend or father. Never having an imaginary friend or a father I spoke to often, this seemed daunting. The house was eerily calm, like the sea before a great storm. I waited in silence and asked for words. When none came, I simply whispered, "Please, God." It felt like enough.

Wednesday nights at church became a safe place to share my feelings. Anna and I sat together, and I burst into tears, "I'm scared," I whispered. Anna squeezed my hand, "I would be, too." She was a good listener, and I was grateful to have a friend. After a few months, Natalie began to drive Amanda to the gatherings. Amanda joined Anna and me in a small group where I asked the leaders to pray for Michelle to come home. They reminded me of the story of the prodigal son, and I thought about my sister, kneeling on all fours, eating from a trough. I could not stomach the thought. *She's a vegetarian, God, please spare her from that humiliation.* When we walked to the doorway, I saw Natalie and Anna's brother, Adam, mingling with a group of older kids. As we passed, Natalie waved to me briefly. I smiled, grateful to be noticed by someone who knew what our family was going through. Natalie walked over to hug me, and I sank into her tall frame, trying not to cry in front of the high schoolers.

The next day, the bus dropped me off at the crossroads of our neighborhood where Amanda, Trevor, and I once rode bikes. I walked alone to the house, enjoying the sunshine. When I opened the door, Michelle was seated on the couch next to a man I immediately recognized. She wore a knitted light-colored hat, and matted hair twists hung to her shoulders. Her face was gaunt. I looked away, quickly walked upstairs to my room, and quietly shut the door. When Britney and I first became friends, we conspired about our siblings getting married so we could be sisters. Seeing Michelle and Britney's half-brother, Rick, on the couch was a distorted lens of our juvenile fantasy. Mom sat opposite them on a chair, and Dad was nowhere in sight. Mom looked weathered thin from counting the days, not hearing from her firstborn. The low hum of conversation expounded for hours. I was a prisoner in my own room, so I opened the window and stepped outside onto the roof, tasting freedom as I sat and waited.

Michelle moved what little stuff she owned back into her bedroom—a pair of Birkenstocks and some old CDs. The prodigal daughter received no fanfare, and I received no explanation. Our family simply moved back into slow rhythms of dinners, with Michelle moving pieces of lettuce around her plate. Dad was quieter these days. Mom prayed, and I joined her under my breath. April picked up the lack of conversation with school accolades and plans for college to pursue the chiropractic trade. As the days passed, Michelle's belly began to protrude from her oversized t-shirts. I figured out Michelle was pregnant without being told. Although approaching thirteen, I still did not know, biologically, how the pregnancy was achieved. Starting my period a couple of months prior, I shut myself in a bathroom, unsure of what was happening to my body. I was sure I was dying, and if not death, something was definitely wrong. Having never been to a doctor before, I imagined our chiropractor could fix whatever was wrong with me during my next visit. A simple adjustment seemed to be the cure for most ailments, except the time April's appendix burst, and she missed her fifth-grade year of school. Mom made her go to softball practice and never forgave herself for mistaking appendicitis for anxiety. Our family did not require vaccinations or medications. Doctors were aptly named "quacks," and hospitals were seen as unnecessary unless it was certain death, like April's situation. Michelle was already planning how to have her baby "naturally," and I shuddered at the thought of what an "unnatural" birth means.

The hushed conversations continued long into the night while I lay awake. My aunt and uncle offered to terminate the pregnancy, and I listened through the cracks in the slatted floors as Mom cried. Drugs were mentioned, and I remembered the tiny green leaves folded inside Michelle's corduroy coat pocket. I pressed my hands together tightly and prayed no drugs would enter the womb where this child was being formed. I prayed away the fear and resentment that lay deep in the pocket of my own belly. I prayed, for the first time, with a desperate hope that this life would have a chance to breathe.

Our family had always held a good faith policy with our neighbors; no one knocked before entering a home. The door was never locked. At some point, in the first few months of Michelle coming home, Rick snuck into the house and stole money from Dad—a cardinal sin. As we sat around the dinner table, Mom blessed our daily meal of venison, potatoes, and salad. Dad ranted about his stock load of guns. We began locking the doors for the first time. Dad threatened to kill Rick if he ever saw him again. I didn't think Dad could do such an act, but I had seen him bring home many dead animals. Because Dad and I had been baptized together and we shared the declaration of now being a Christian, I could not justify his words. We were told that after we accepted Jesus into our hearts, we were to be "holy and blameless." Dad's words were filled with rage and hatred. I had never had a pregnant teenage daughter, though, so I could not possibly understand. A great sadness filled me to think about Michelle raising her baby without the baby knowing his father. At every family gathering, Dad said, "Family is the most important thing." I sipped in the pride, knowing I had a role to play in helping however I could. I vowed not to have sex until I was married. I vowed to be good. I vowed not to cause any trouble in our home. I vowed to support our family, no matter if it cost me my friendships.

The new middle school had not yet been built, so a row of trailers was placed like train cars lining the back of the local high school. Britney and I drifted apart as the news of Michelle's pregnancy circulated throughout the hallways. With fierce loyalty to my family, pride built a cage to keep my sadness inside. I stayed after class to help the teachers organize their papers or borrowed books to avoid passing Britney and her new group of friends. I stayed distracted by my relationship with Daniel, spending time talking on the phone with him daily, attending movies on the weekends, and attending parties. He snuck poetry into my locker, and we reenacted Shakespeare's "The Tragedy of Romeo and Juliet" for a school play. When we discovered we had separate classes that semester, I was determined nothing would change.

One day, I entered the cafeteria, passing rows of blue plastic chairs. Former friends lowered their gaze. I spotted Daniel with Britney's new best friend, Jenna. Daniel glanced my way and looked around for an open chair, but there were none. He shrugged his shoulders and continued his conversation with Jenna. I stood trembling; my hands shook so badly I nearly dropped my lunch. I walked to the courtyard, rounded the corner, and pressed my back against the brick wall, exhaling fully as I slid onto the concrete slab. My chest burned, and my stomach wrapped tightly in knots. Staring at the blur of high schoolers' cars, I allowed the weight of pain to move through my body. Tears formed, and anger swelled. I gritted my teeth and dried my eyes with the end of my sleeve. *I won't let them see me like this.* I tossed my lunch into the open trash can and took a different route to class. The next day, I quit eating in the cafeteria and went outside to sit in the courtyard, taking my journal and a pen. After a few weeks, I quit eating lunch. In solitude, my journal became an outlet of words instead of tears, hidden from the world around me. Food became an enemy I could control.

I began to notice a few of Natalie's high school friends and said hello as I passed by in the gym or during dismissal. Eventually, they began to wave when they saw me around the school. On the weekends, I invited myself to Amanda and Natalie's house, ignoring Amanda. When Natalie began to drive, I asked her for a ride home from school, hoping Britney or Daniel saw me as they entered their buses.

A chill was in the air as I sauntered to band class from the classroom trailers. The loudspeaker crackled, "Mr. Collins. Can you please send Christine to the front office?"

I jumped from the chair and yelled, "My sister is having her baby!" I grabbed my backpack and clarinet and ran down the hallway through the double doors.

Dad's work van was parked in the front of the building. I hoisted myself up onto the leather seat. The van smelled of grease and oranges. He lit a cigarette as we sped away to meet our newest family member. When I arrived at the hospital, it was sterile and smelled thick of astringent. A tiny swaddle was put into my arms, a blue hat covering a curl of dark hair. I immediately fell in love with this tiny creature in a way that no boyfriend could touch. The blanket grew warm beneath my arms, and we all laughed as Braxton and I began our relationship, peed on.

The first year of Braxton's life was marred by back-and-forth custody battles to determine who could love the child most. In the end, Michelle proved that her newfound identity as a mother was the strongest form of love. Barely twenty and a single mom, she gave herself to sleepless nights, breastfeeding, job hunting, and strengthening the legs beneath her. College textbooks collected dust as she pushed forward, disproving every negative word spoken over her. Braxton's life closed a chapter of struggle and set a tone of unity within our home. He became my little buddy, my source of pride as an aunt. From the first steps to t-ball games, being Aunt Kei-Kei (because "Chris-tine" is just too difficult for a toddler) instilled a sense of worth. Dad stepped in quickly to fill the space Rick had left in Braxton's life. He drank a little less and started a men's group with some folks from the church. The emptiness of not having a son to call Seth Michael dissipated as each month with Braxton passed. A renewed sense of belonging sprouted beneath the bosom of each family member as we learned to love one another despite the brokenness of circumstances.

Time moved slowly as molasses in the South. Years passed quietly. Outside, the darkness engulfed the town, even amidst the scattered stars. Like freckles down summer shoulders, the stars intricately punctuated and became a mass of softened light in the same breath. Still, the dim and the glow could not keep out the dark. There was nothing to distract me from growing up except myself.

During Algebra, a classmate noticed the picture of Braxton on my binder—wide-mouthed grin, squinting his eyes against the sun. His toddler's hands held up two branches as his imaginary drumsticks.

She leaned over, close to my ear, "Who is Braxton's dad?" Without hesitation, I replied, "He doesn't have a dad; he has a sperm donor."

Her face lost expression as she pulled her body back into the sanctuary of her desk. We both turned toward the whiteboard, where Mrs. Hancock continued lecturing.

During my next class, the speaker clicked on, "Sorry to interrupt, but can you send Christine to the front office, please?" Within a half hour of my comment, Britney burst into tears in the middle of the hallway, creating a scene around her so everyone nearby heard my comment about her brother. *Middle school drama queen*, I think to myself. The principal glared at me beneath a halo of frizzy hair.

"Do you have anything to say for yourself?" she asked.

"No, ma'am," I growled slowly, attempting to keep my stubbornness polite.

Mrs. Hancock pressed, "It has been brought to my attention that you have said unkind things about Britney's family. Is this true?"

My face was set like a flint. I bit hard on the side of my cheek, deliberating on my response.

"I did not say anything that I don't believe is true," the flat, harshness of my tone surprised me.

"That is very disrespectful. I think it would be wise for you to see our school counselor. Have a seat," Mrs. Hancock retorted as she turned and walked down the hallway toward her office.

Britney was one of her favorite students, having been chosen to sing and perform for multiple school events. I shifted indifferently in my chair, puffing up my chest to defend our family. I had snuck April's jacket to school that day, so I felt tough behind the starchy leather exterior. *Heaven forbid Mom finds out I was sent to the principal. She doesn't need anything else to worry about these days.*

The counselor was a young, beautiful woman with deep brown skin. She had bright, wide lips and dark eyes. She welcomed me to sit down. Instead of asking why I was there, she inquired, "How are you doing?" I sat silently for a few minutes, considering the paths to take this conversation. In her presence, I felt a sense of calm soften my shoulders. I took a deep, cleansing breath and began sharing my story. I told her what I had only written in my journal. She asked about the pain of losing my friends and first love and how I felt about having a baby in our home. For the first time, my ears clung to words only spoken in my mind. It felt natural and good, this outpouring. I began to cry, letting the tears finally release, not needing to stay strong for anyone.

"I've stopped eating," I confessed. "Everything feels out of control, and I feel alone."

After speaking, I exhaled deeply and sat, waiting for the verdict. *Am I still lovable?* The counselor looked at me with gentleness and began to speak softly. Her voice wavered a bit as tears sprung from her own deep pain. She shared a moment with me, an insecurity born from her past childhood. She told me about her experiences in middle school, and I felt known as we sat with one another. It was a sacred space, this shared union. *Someone understands.* In the risk of breaking silence, vulnerability became a mutual exchange in which healing was invited to enter the crack in my heart. The dormant words of anger that clamored throughout the walls of our home took shape as a seed of bitter resentment, now peeking through the surface. "You're not alone in your feelings," she assured me as we said our goodbyes. She invited me to come back and see her whenever I wanted to, but I knew I never would. The exposure felt too painful.

The sun's radiance brightly streaked and bounced from the rims of the rattling buses. Heat emitted from the tarmac, wearing through the soles of our shoes. A group of middle and high school students stood outside the church carrying headphones and pillows and oversized t-shirts, barely covering the girls' shorts. I looked down at my legs, embarrassed by how stocky they seemed standing next to Natalie's tall and slender frame. She was a blonde goddess next to my 5 foot 3 shape, topped with ashy brown hair. Natalie insisted I borrow a pair of her cheerleading shorts. Standing amidst the other high school girls, I regretted my decision to say yes.

During the past year, my breasts had grown to compensate for my lack of height or beauty. A few boys at school made a game of talking about them without getting in trouble, telling me how much they wanted to climb "the Grand Tetons" or sit behind me to unhook my bra in the middle of class. The boys in Natalie's group of friends were a few years older than I was, but they didn't seem to mind the middle school girl. They didn't look at me like the boys in my grade did, and I was thankful to feel unseen. From years of Dad's outbursts, I learned the art of invisibility. Given the climate instability in our home, I developed the art of speaking only when spoken to. I was rarely spoken to, so I learned to laugh at others' jokes and smile. *Easy enough.* The newly formed relationship between Anna's brother, Adam, and Natalie bridged the age gap in our friend groups. I was excited about the trip to Florida for my first youth group retreat experience. It was my first time away from home without Mom coming along as a chaperone. As we waited to board the buses, a large guy with shaggy brown hair pulled out his guitar and began singing George Michael's *Faith*. As two or three more people chimed in, I sang a few lines of the chorus I knew and felt I might fit in nicely with this group.

      Our sweaty bodies crowded into the narrow aisles of the rented charter bus. Outdated patterns slashed throughout the soft fabric seats. I tried to stay close to Natalie, but she found a seat with a dark-haired girl I recognized from our Wednesday night gatherings. Anna was stuck outside the back of the line, so I plopped my pillow down into an open space to wait for her. Before I had situated my backpack on the floorboard, I turned in my chair to find Alex beside me. I had seen him at Anna's house several times when I spent the night. Alex and Adam were always upstairs in the bonus room playing the guitar or video games. We never spoke, but I knew who he was from those brief interactions. I caught Anna's eye from the back of the line and shrugged my shoulders, mouthing *sorry*. She smiled back and found an open seat with her cousin in the front of the bus.

      Alex's mop of red hair covered the freckles that lined the back of his pale neck. His gangly legs, covered mainly by the oversized shorts he wore, splayed in the aisle. Alex joked loudly with the other high school kids who had taken over the back of the charter bus. The boisterous laughter swayed into shuffling backpacks and crinkling candy wrappers as the seats filled. Alex turned his body toward mine, bumping his knee into my leg, "Hey, Christine."

"Uh, hey . . . Alex. I didn't realize you knew my name." He laughed, large lines curved deeply into his cheeks like the Cheshire Cat waiting to tell the next riddle. Alex's teeth were stained with a dull tint of yellow that matched his translucent skin. Green pupils shined mischievously from beneath his rust-colored eyelashes. I breathed deeply, suddenly remembering my exposed legs jolting from Natalie's shorts like two plump sausages. The group leader for the girls gave a long talk on modesty before the trip. She reminded us we were not allowed to wear inappropriate bathing suits or any clothes that were too revealing to not cause the boys on the trip to sin by lusting. My mom agreed to take me shopping for a bathing suit shaped more like a tank top; I could pull it all the way down my torso to not expose my stomach. Natalie told me this was the loophole, so I didn't have to wear a one-piece. The same guy who began the expedition with his rendition of *Faith* began to play guitar again, and the gentle roar of teenage hormones cut through the crowd as Alex glanced at my shirt. I pretended not to notice and looked out the window as the parking lot emptied and the bus rolled onto the road.

Alex leaned over the seat, talking to the girls across the aisle. They laughed as he shared stories from the videos of bottle rocket wars and exploding watermelons he and Adam made. I settled into his presence and laughed along, feeling the weight of home lessen with each mile marker we passed. When Alex began playing his guitar, I was happy to know a few songs and sang along. Stoicism rooted in the *good girl, high achiever, stay quiet* persona peeled back for a moment, and I felt like the other kids. There was no nephew to rock to sleep, no unpredictable father to avoid, and no grade to strive for to hear, "Well done!" I felt the world was made right an hour into our five-hour drive. Maybe this Jesus really did love me.

When we stopped for lunch, I quickly stood and walked off the bus to find Anna in the crowd. "How are things going?" I heard her voice from behind me.

"I'm having a lot of fun, surprisingly. Alex is really funny," I shared.

"Yeah, he's crazy," she replied before changing the subject. "I've been getting my beauty sleep," Anna dramatically batted her eyelashes. "Stephanie is trying to talk to me about this boy she really likes at school. It's really annoying. She keeps talking and talking and talking." Her voice lowered to a whisper, and she looked around to ensure Stephanie was not within earshot before stating, "I don't think he likes her."

"Oh man, that's rough," I shrugged.

"How have you been doing?" Anna asked. Her long blonde ponytail swished as she sat down in an available booth.

I took the seat next to her. "Fine. Everyone is just listening to music, so I borrowed some CDs from Natalie." Anna looked at my empty hands while unloading her french fries and burger tray onto the dirty table. "Are you getting anything to eat?" she asked. "I ate before I came," I lied. "Still full." Middle school and my choice of skinny friends had only exacerbated my fear of eating in front of other people. Anna shrugged indifferently and took a big bite of her cheeseburger, ketchup oozing from the side.

Back on the bus, guitar karaoke and card playing had turned into napping and listening to music through headphones. Some kids who didn't suffer from car sickness took out their books to read. I borrowed another CD from Natalie and resumed listening to an angst-filled musician when Alex's body shifted closer to mine. Instinctively, my head turned away from the window where I had been lazily enjoying the scenery blur past. I looked at him, but he did not look back in my direction. I was embarrassed that I would consider it more than accidental. Feeling exposed, I reached for my pillow and rested it on my lap.

My leg instinctively twitched, startled by Alex's milk-white hand moving toward my waistband. Like a thief outside the window deliberating the consequences of trespassing, he proceeded to slide his hand beneath my underwear. Alex stole what was never his to take with no regard to whose body it belonged. My chest heaved in my body as I held my breath, trying not to make a sound. His fingers curved between my legs, pressing into me. I swallowed hard. Heat radiated from my cheeks down to my neck, moving through my hands into the ends of my fingertips. I wanted to stand up and run away, to scream, "Stop!" but I was paralyzed. I resolved to stare at the clouds and unkempt yards, dogs panting from the summer haze. I focused on my breath to keep from crying, to remind myself I was still alive. The muscles in my thighs contracted, and Alex removed his hand, having his fill of violating the parts of me meant for consent. The pleasure in my body was as thick as the guilt, the language of self-betrayal. My voice caught in my throat like the curse of the sea witch. Shame swam through my veins, a mermaid of the dark.

The expanse of time between a middle school girl and a soon-to-be man weighed heavy in the air. I hated him. I hated myself.

The bus lurched to a stop. Without a look or word, Alex stood and moved away. Embarrassment pervaded as the damp heat remained. I glared as the last rays of light dipped into the lapping waves, wondering how letting the salt water fill my lungs would feel. I was emptied. Slowly, my breath returned as the ocean's pull reminded me to breathe. I resolved never to wear shorts again.

As Natalie walked past, I tried to lift the sides of my cheeks to smile, but the muscles groaned under the weight. I filled my lungs and held the air at the top until the piercing sensation slowed my exhalation, knowing I must learn what it feels like to be human again. Slowly, movement re-entered my fingers. I watched myself pick up my backpack from the ground, but it was as if the hand belonged to someone else. The ghost of my image appeared on the window pane. I traced the outline of my eyes as they filled with ocean water. I held back the tears, biting my lip hard. I wanted to be a child again, to curl up into Dad's arms and cry. I wanted Dad to lock the doors that kept Rick from stealing from our home and would protect me from Alex stealing from the temple of my body.

I moved slowly from the seat, shuffling into the shared room of the hotel with Anna and a few other girls I knew from church. I told her I was tired and placed the pillow on top of the bed, hiding underneath the weight of the covers. When the others left for dinner, I was free to cry. No tears formed. I stared, motionless, for hours until my body gave way and sleep graced my mind. In the morning, the fog of my brain began to lift. My body felt awkwardly thick, and I stripped my clothes to change into the tank-top-shaped bathing suit. I stared down at my body, and I did not recognize my own form. In my shame, I reached for the proverbial leaves of my swimsuit and pulled hard on the fabric to ensure my stomach was fully covered.

    The camp was filled with enough activities to keep the incident in the back of my mind. It stayed as a low hum, always present. When we were given free time, I sat by the ocean and watched the tide sweep away patterns of shells and crabs, tiny exoskeletons lining the path. Parts of my worth collapsed with each passing of Alex. In quiet moments, when no one was around, he would slink over, close enough for me to feel his presence. He walked beside me, brushing an arm gently across my shoulders out of sight from the others. When I moved closer, he slipped away into a group of people, always watching. We ebbed and flowed. From across the room, Alex caught my eye. He winked with the same cat smile that once held something of light. I wanted to smash his teeth. I wanted him to say something to validate or turn this darkness into light. I wanted him to apologize, acknowledge the weight of his decision, and tell me it was not my fault. Nothing came, so I mimicked the rhythm of the crowd, losing myself to find stability in the strength of others. When I was with Anna, I found the parts of me that felt lost. I began to laugh again, to feel the normality of my body's movements. When Alex entered the space, the familiar sensations left my body as if I were floating with no form. The pattern continued. Alex, close enough so I could feel his breath on the back of my neck, whispering, "Hey, you . . ." Approaching me publicly, only when I was with Anna, Alex continued inviting us to join his group of friends to walk on the beach. Anna encouraged me to participate in the frivolity, giggling as we splashed through the shallow waves that pulled toward our feet. We found a large piece of driftwood and scattered ourselves on top. Boys and girls began to pair up. Alex pulled out his guitar from the case and sang a few songs I had heard on the radio in Natalie's car. Anna glanced my way and smiled. She sat next to a curly blond-haired boy. I raised my eyebrows and laughed at her as we began singing along. My eyes darted toward Alex, and he looked my way, continuing to lead us through the melody. My body grew warm.

    Anna turned toward me, "Do you like him?" she whispered.

    Instinctively, I shook my head no.

On the last morning of camp, we dragged our weary bodies to the parking lot, where the same two buses emerged from around the corner. I felt my stomach turn as they pulled in front of the hotel. Frantically, I looked around the sea of faces to find Anna. She was standing by the door, pillow in hand. I grabbed my bag and rushed toward her.

"Will you please sit with me on the way home?" I exhaled.

"Sure, let me just tell my cousin." Anna rolled her eyes, "I'm not sure that she made any other friends here, so I kinda feel bad."

"I get it, but I really, really don't want to sit with anyone else. Is that okay?" I pleaded.

"Yeah, of course. She'll be fine. Just give me a sec'."

Anna pushed her pillow into my chest and walked into the crowd to deliver her seating arrangement to her cousin. Laughter burst from behind me as the doors opened. I could feel Alex before he touched me, playfully nudging me forward as he passed. I watched the back of his frame march up the stairs and onto the bus ahead. When Anna returned, I clutched her pillow and led us to the bus opposite the one Alex had chosen. The ride home was quiet as my mind recounted the trip's events. I attempted to make sense of my desire to have Alex close while still hating how he made me feel inside.

A few days passed before Anna invited me to spend the night at her house. Considering Alex's possibility of being there, I fixed my hair and picked out clothes from my sister's closet. When I arrived to find no one there except Anna and her mom, disappointment settled in. I sat on the couch waiting for Anna to finish getting ready while her mom left for the grocery store. Adam's car pulled into the driveway, and I froze. Alex entered from the side door, walked toward me without hesitation, and plopped on the same cushion.

Looking into my eyes for the first time, he asked, "How are you?" Alex did not reach his arm around me or pull me into him. He did not touch me at all except for the outline of his body pressed against the side of mine. Alex smiled, and I drowned in the riptide of a desire awakened by someone I did not choose. Adam laughed and walked upstairs to his room.

"Good," I shrugged. "I didn't know you were going to be here."

"Well," he smiled, revealing his stained teeth, "I thought you might be here."

My heart began to race.

"You don't even talk to me," I replied.

"Sure I do! We spent the whole week together at camp," he leaned his shoulder into mine.

As Adam bounded down the stairs, Alex stood to leave, and I was a vapor.

In the months following our encounter, I anticipated Alex's presence at church or when I spent time with Anna. I never knew if I would be acknowledged again. Waves of attention from Alex were followed quickly by the withdrawal back into the sea of his friends, much older and different than my own. Darkness became a cloak around my sulking shoulders as I retreated into my writing. I transfigured gruesome thoughts into poetry, flashbacks turned into metaphors. Even in sleep, my mind did not rest. Nightmares gripped me, and I woke drenched in sweat. Demons began to manifest. I took a sharp knife labeled "Heavenly" and dug into my flesh, praying to feel something against the numbness. The point drove into my skin enough to leave a mark but not enough to draw immediate attention to scars. I avoided people, still aching to be noticed. I found Alex's number when the burden became too heavy to hold. Manic and in tears, I heard my voice scratch over the receiver, "Who do you think I am? Am I just some . . . girl to you? Just someone you can use and never speak to again?" *Just a thirteen-year-old girl.* I could not say my age. I already felt the weight of my child-like behavior by calling Alex unannounced and crying. The words hung in the pause like a lifetime of silent resentment shot through.

"I really like you," came the response.

The anger shapeshifted into confusion.

"You don't know me," I croaked. "You never even speak to me around other people." My voice grew louder with an unexpected boldness.

"I know. I think you're pretty cool, though," Alex responded. "Listen, you're not just some girl to me, but I can't talk right now. I've got to go."

I heard the click of the other line. I was bewildered at his sentiment as the conversation ended abruptly.

In an act of desperation or self-pity, I called Alex again. I was standing on the roof, ready to jump this time. My confession to the priest became a self-fulfilled prophecy. Again came the response, "I really care about you." And added, "Don't do this," to cover his guilt. When we hung up the phone, I crawled back through my window from the rooftop. I could not make sense of the tears or this feeling of weightlessness. I grabbed a bag from the closet and pulled out a bottle of bubbles left over from a wedding I attended. Sitting on the wooden floor of my room, I traced the eyes of the monsters staring back at me. I dipped the wand into the liquid, lifting the plastic circle to my lips. I inhaled deeply and exhaled fully as I watched each bubble rise. Each one refracted a glorious promise of God captured in a rainbow of colors and ended in a resounding and satisfying POP!

The next time I saw Alex, he was standing with a group of guys on the trip with us. I expected him to move, come closer, say I'm sorry, or say hello. There was no response to our telephone conversation. The torture of the game compounded as my adolescent mind became transfixed on Alex. His physical touch had awakened an intense desire to connect with him, even though I knew he didn't care about me. I gave into the false sense of connectivity. Innocence stripped, I craved meaning that extended past abuse. I could still feel Alex's hand on me, and I wanted to remove my skin.

Testing the shallow end of the waters, I began asking the pastor at our church small questions about the lack of supervision and the mix of middle and high school kids on retreats. No one listened with sincerity. Hoping for someone to understand, I stayed after church ended on Sunday and asked if I could speak to a female small group leader. When I opened my mouth to talk, it was filled with the taste of shame, and I did not have adequate language to convey what I experienced with Alex.

"He touched me," I heard myself say. Like a word bubble lingering in the air, I watched the words float up and out of my mouth, but they did not hold weight. I wanted to grab hold of them and bring them back inside, allowing the silence to remain. My body was numb as I waited for a response.

The young woman was quiet momentarily, "What kind of touch?" My eyes fell to my shoes, unaware of how to proceed. I had never had a man touch me before. Assuming this older woman would somehow formulate words for me to give language to my experience, I was left with only a greater sense of shame. *Touch that makes your whole body feel alive and, in the same breath, hate yourself and feel disconnected from every person around you because you did not ask to receive it. What kind of touch is that?* I thought to myself.

"I don't know," I muttered. I saw her head move to the side as she awaited my response. I remained silent as my brain replayed the incident until my body felt outside. She patted me on the hand and said she would pray for me.

Without an appetite or sleep, my body became thin. With April at college, I pulled the bunk beds apart in my bedroom and left a single mattress on the floor. I lined my room with candles and spent hours alone writing. Some days, I caught the wind from the rooftop. I let it move my hair around, so I knew movement was happening, even if it was only outside myself. I blew bubbles to remind myself I was alive. My mind drifted to falling from the roof, wondering who would attend my funeral. Would Alex come? Would God still invite me into Heaven? I dragged the pocket knife into my skin, pressing in more deeply to leave a mark. When I saw the red lines form with no pain present, I was aware I needed to say something to someone else. There is something wrong with my body.

Dad was asleep in the chair when I asked Mom if we could talk. As we sat across the kitchen table, I inhaled deeply.

"I think I am depressed," I said plainly.

"Christine, you know that you accepted Jesus in your heart. When you do that, he will bring you joy. Just keep asking him!" She stood, walked around the table, and placed her arm around me. I could not feel her weight on my skin. I had stones around my heart, shutting out those around me. No one felt safe.

Alex graduated the summer before I began high school, and I never saw him again.

Chapter 4

A boy exited through the open door, examining the stairs that tumbled down in front of the newly constructed high school building. We exchanged glances. My eyes darted away, staring at the cross of laces zig-zagging down my stark white Adidas. The boy sat on the stairs adjacent to me before looking over his shoulder in my direction.

"Hey, I think I've seen you around. I just moved here, so I'm still trying to figure things out." He told me his name was Jake.

"But what's your real name, your birth name?" The words fumbled from my lips. Jake smiled, his wide mouth revealing a large row of white teeth.

"Jacob Andrew, but no one has called me that since third grade," he said, laughing a little.

"Well, maybe I will start calling you that now." My abrupt response surprised me, and I noticed myself smiling too.

Jake was noticeably different from the other boys I'd grown accustomed to in Sharpsburg. His hair was spiked upward and streaked with platinum blonde tips. Jake wore skateboarding shoes and a t shirt displaying a punk band name across the front in large block letters.

"My family just moved here from Philly. Dad got a new job." Jake fumbled with his backpack strap.

"What does your dad do for work?" I asked.

"I don't know. He sells medical equipment or something like that." When Jake looked up, I felt my face flush with warmth.

"Medical equipment? I don't really know what that means," I confessed, embarrassed. "I've only been to a hospital once, when my sister's appendix burst." The muscles of my face tensed, remembering April's pale skin, tubes, and machines pulsing around her small frame.

"Man, is she ok?" Jake's eyebrows raised.

"Oh, sorry! Yes, she's fine," I laughed nervously.

"You've been to the doctor though ... you know, the kind of stuff they use there. That's the kind of stuff my dad sells."

In a continuum of truth-telling, I shook my head. "No, actually, I've never been to the doctor." I shrugged my shoulders.

"What? That's crazy. So, do you just not get sick or what?" Jake asked.

"I mean, it's just kind of normal for us. Mom makes us drink apple cider vinegar and take vitamins when we get sick. I see a chiropractor, so I guess I have been to a doctor." His face looked at mine inquisitively, and I felt exposed beneath his gaze. Steering the conversation onto a different course, "So, tell me about Philly. I can't imagine moving from a big city like that to Sharpsburg. Must be hard."

"Yeah," Jake looked away. "It's not easy making friends here. People are kinda ...," his voice trailed off. "It's not that people are rude, they're just not ... like you, I guess."

"What do you mean, like *me*?" I interjected.

"Open." He shrugged. "Nice."

My face flushed, and I glanced back down toward my shoes.

"There's my mom," Jake pointed to the white car in line, and he stood to leave. He turned around quickly, "I could give you my handle, and we can keep talking online if you want."

"Sure," I said casually, reaching for my pen.

Jake took the pen from my hand, gently turning my palm over. He pressed the ink into my wrist, where my eyes darted toward the tiny scars etched on my forearm. I swallowed hard, hoping he didn't notice.

"I'll jump on the computer when I get home and leave it on if you want to chat." He placed the pen back into my hand and shuffled his backpack over one shoulder, bounding down the remainder of the steps. As the car drove past, I saw his hand raise to wave and a flash of his smile. I turned my hand over to see a symbol and a few letters written on my arm, renaming the scars. I took a deep breath, and I was grateful to feel again.

When the bus stopped, I ran down the street into an empty house. My bookbag splayed open beside my chair as I waited for the computer screen to appear against the dark backdrop. Typing in each letter slowly, I held my breath until a text popped onto the screen. The conversation began with all the emotions our teenage minds can only awkwardly express. We talked about school, friends, where he has been, and the names of his favorite bands. Sitting behind a screen, I boldly typed details of my life I would not have felt confident enough to express face to face. I laughed at his responses, and it felt good to smile.

I held onto each word on the screen, wanting to bottle all of his experiences. I lived them out in my imagination. Lost in a world of tall buildings and hurried streets, I imagined I could throw back time and trade places with him for just a day. I wanted to feel the excitement of living outside this Godforsaken town, with its same faces and buried secrets.

The next day at school, I looked for Jake in the halls between classes. When I didn't see him, I stared at the clock, waiting for the school day to end so we could get on the computer and talk some more. At lunch, I found a seat alone in the courtyard to avoid the question of why I was not eating. Some days, I sat and watched other people congregate. I listened to them laugh or tell jokes, wondering about their true life story. A group of students huddled together when a spontaneous dance began, cheers exploding from the outer circle. An administrator hustled to quiet them and was reassured that no misbehavior had ensued, only dancing. I brought a journal and enjoyed a quiet moment with my thoughts. Mostly, I just sat alone and hoped someone noticed.

Jake found me at the football game on Friday night and stood close. "I looked for you in the hallway, but I haven't seen you at all this week."

"I know. I mean, me too," I stumbled. "I didn't see you either," I landed awkwardly.

"I was hoping you'd want to come over tomorrow. We can walk to a lake behind my house or watch a movie or something." His hands remained jammed inside his pockets as we stared at the football field.

"Yeah, that sounds fun." I tried to measure my words evenly. "Who else is coming?"

"No one," Jake replied, quickly following up, "I mean, if you're okay with that."

"Yeah," I tried to remain calm, "of course." I felt my face growing warm and stared down at my shoes. My toes turned inward as they often did when I felt insecure. I bit down hard on the inside of my cheek, the taste of metal coating my tongue.

When Michelle and April were in high school, there were strict rules in our home about boys not coming into our bedrooms or being in the house without a parent home. Whether it was because of Braxton's birth or because of my baptism, the same rules, somehow, didn't apply to me. When the Y2K scare happened in middle school, our friends gathered to build a time capsule. We stayed up all night watching movies and fell asleep with our boyfriends once the sun rose. I had been to plenty of "chaperoned" parties, sneaking out of my friend's houses after their parents fell asleep to kiss boys in the neighborhood or play Truth or Dare. Most of my friends' parents knew what was happening and would joke about it with us the following day over pancakes.

I saw people having sex for the first time the night my friend dared to bring down a magazine from her brother's room. It was dark outside; the street lamp lights illuminated the glossy bodies.

A knot formed in my stomach as we huddled around, turning page after page. "Why would anyone want to do that?" I whispered, scrunching up my nose and turning away.

"I don't know," another friend responded, "but it looks fun." She laughed.

"No way," I said, remembering how the actors were saturated with warm light in the movies I had seen. "Anyway, I'm not having sex until I'm married, so I guess I'll just figure it out then."

Having witnessed Michelle's life change in order to raise Braxton, I knew whatever sex was, I was not ready to have a baby. And whatever it was in that magazine did not make me want to risk it. My desire to be a good Christian was magnified by the fear of getting pregnant as if the two went hand in hand. After the incident with Alex, I had no interest in letting any boy touch me again. I found the illusion of goodness in the form of abstinence and held on tightly.

Jake and I walked hand in hand the next day, fishing poles dangling behind our backs. As we cut through a small trail behind his house, I imagined Maggie's forbidden castle looming through the trees. Instead, a modest white house with a small deck overlooking the lake came into view.

"Mr. Hogan lives here," Jake cut through my memory. "He's a nice old man who told me when we moved in this summer that I could come and fish any time I want. Sometimes, I just come here to sit and write songs."

"I didn't know you wrote," I paused to look down at our hands still clasped tightly. As we stepped onto the wooden slats of the dock, I reluctantly loosened my grip. Jake held a fishing rod, and I cast the line onto the rippling waves. I removed my socks and shoes, dangling my slender feet over the edge. The voice of my dad laughed in my ear, *you could ski without skis with those feet!* I considered putting my socks back on but chose to stay seated so as not to bring more attention to them.

The pole line whispered out to the water with a satisfying *plink*. Jake's body sank into mine as he settled himself beside me. My arm tensed involuntarily, breath catching in my chest. In a flash of panic, I looked behind me to see a barricade of trees and only the lake ahead. Formulating an exit strategy, I decided to take the driveway path to the nearest road and wave for someone to pull over and drive me home. I looked over to see the profile of Jake's square jaw, soft eyes gazing toward the floating bobber.

He turned toward me and smiled, "You okay?"

"Yeah. Yes. I'm okay," I choked. I took a full breath, holding the air at the top of my shoulders to feel the muscles squeeze together, and exhaled deeply, releasing my shoulders away from my ears. I noticed my free hand pressed into a tight fist. Sipping in more air, I released my grasp and reached for Jake's hand. He squeezed it gently, and I settled my body into the side of his. The sun beat down upon us as we exposed our skin to the heat. I was enamored and entirely taken by the slightest hint of attention.

The summer lull came with mischief in its eyes, and we embraced it fully. We kissed as though we had never tasted the lips of another. I gently swayed back and forth, like a fish released, learning to breathe again in the safety of these waters.

Our friends joined us for summer days wasted at the pool and trips to the lake house with Jake's family. Jake and I were asked to lead the youth worship band at church. We spent our time together writing songs. He played guitar while I sang along. My childhood dreams were reimagined on a much smaller stage filled with the grandeur of lights and sound systems. Jake and I snuck our way into louder and bigger churches. We absorbed new ideas for our writing while spending the rest of our hours melding into one another. In the evenings, we stayed enclosed in the safety of the church walls. Our leaders often reminded us of sin's consequences and the rewards of purity and holiness.

The unanswerable question behind every do-good Christian high school student was finally asked aloud, "How far is too far?"

From the pastor, the suggestion resounded, "If you keep your feet on the ground, you should be fine." Confused and slightly humored, I thought, *That's not helpful. I can do a lot of things with my feet on the ground!*

Days turned into months that stretched lazily into the following year. Jake and I spent ourselves on every teenage emotion. Each dance, football game, church event, or vacation was painted over with the intensity of our conversations and the wandering of hands and lips. Jake became the standard to measure all other men in my life. In the sanctuary of his arms, I traced the boundaries of my body. There, I knew I was safe to explore. There was no yes without my consent. I found strength in keeping my standard of purity as the expectation for our relationship. My "no" was my power, and I wielded a sword around it to keep me from being hurt again.

Behind the town library, Jake and I sat beneath the arms of a large oak tree. Over the last year, this secluded park of wild clover had afforded us the opportunity to perfect the art of kissing. When his hand reached the button of my jeans, I pulled away. My mind carried me to the bus, Alex's bony fingers, and the awakening of this same feeling. I was scared and ashamed. Warm tears formed as I clenched my eyes shut, my body materializing into stone. We sat with silence between us, our bodies expanding and contracting with every pulse of each other's breath and weight.

"I'm a virgin," I whispered, our foreheads still pressed together.

"That's okay," his chest rising and falling with mine.

"No, I mean . . ." I clamored for words. "I am going to stay a virgin until I am married."

Jake traced the line on the lower space of my jaw with his finger, gently pulling my gaze up to hold his, "I won't do anything you are uncomfortable doing."

"Thank you," I exhaled. Safe in his presence again, my body relaxed.

"Christine," his breath warmed my cheek, "I love you. I'll never hurt you."

Rolling onto his side, Jake pointed to the large wicker basket holding down the corner of our quilt. He grinned, "Why don't you look inside?"

I slowed my breathing to bring feeling back into my fingers and evaporate the tears from my eyelids.

"C'mon," Jake persisted. "Open the basket!"
I turned my eyes toward the clouded blue sky, the giving tree bent down in service. Reaching into the basket, a tiny box nestled next to sandwiches and a soda. I looked at Jake, pursing my lips inquisitively. Inside the box resided a small silver band with a cross detailed in the middle.

"I hope it's the right size," he said. "It's a promise ring."

My eyes were lakes. I smiled quickly before thrusting the ring on my finger and barreling into him. Jake fell backward and kissed me hard. "This is a reminder we will stay pure before God until we are married," he said into my hair.

"Happy one-year anniversary," I grinned through the tears. "I love you."

My face flushed; I rolled to my back and closed my eyes. I was trembling. *This is what it feels like to be alive. To be loved.*

There was only darkness when I sat upright in bed, the warmth of the comforter weighed down my legs. The lights in the house had been extinguished for hours, and the only sliver now was from the moon, shining white through the window in my room. My eyelids were heavy, poised for sleep. I heard the sound of Mom's voice calling my name. My feet thumped softly against the hardwood floor, and I stepped into the hallway. My hands lazily traveled across the walls, revealing the light switch to the upstairs entry.

"I'm here," I beckoned to the open air; my voice traveled down the stairs in response to the call. Descending a few steps, I paused and waited. Silence lingered. I tuned into the song of cicadas reverberating among the trees outside these walls. The stars beamed inward through the huge glass panes lining the adjacent wall. There was a mystery here in this log cabin Dad built. Each groove and room had a story to share, a family to protect, and secrets to tell. Downstairs, nothing was illuminated. No one stirred in the dead hours tonight. Still hazy from the sudden awakening, I lifted my feet from the wooden slats beneath me, backed up the stairs, and climbed into the covers. The sheets enveloped my small frame, and I sank into the familiar comfort.

The voice called again.

Just one word.

My name.

Clearly. Distinctly.

Christine.

Without opening my eyes, I settled into the moment. My heart rushed and felt full of life. The sound was sweet. This voice——the One who knows me. He was the One who formed me and knit me in my Mother's womb.

This was not Mom's voice.

This was the voice of my Heavenly Father.

I smiled.

With this peaceful realization still washing over me, my body surrendered to deep rest.

To be known and not loved was the fear that kept me from risking true intimacy with another. To be loved and not known is a lonely sickness that thrives on fantasy. To be *known and loved* was my greatest longing and the space where my truest self could shine radiantly.

    I merged myself into Jake, hoping his love could sustain us both. Creating a space of deep intimacy while maintaining our commitment to one another to abstain from having sex became a constant source of pain. I placed more rules around our time together, hoping the temptation would leave. I prayed I could become better at "guarding my heart," which I mistook for killing my God-given sexual desire. The pressure of purity left us both strained, vacillating between letting each other go completely or fast-tracking toward marriage.

    As Jake's hands wandered too far, I fell back into depression, knowing we had chosen to move past the boundaries of our own making. Seizing as I cried on the bathroom floor, my mind reverted to the memories of Alex. Between my desire to remain pure and the confusion of living in the liminal space of intimacy, our relationship turned into a blur of confusion. Out of fear and anger, I told him I needed a break from our relationship for a few months. I challenged Jake's commitment to make sure we remained pure before God, scared I was already too far damaged to be accepted. I reminded him of what the church had told us about the role of men in the Bible, handing over all responsibility for our actions.

    Midway through my senior year, I received an early acceptance letter to the state university, my first invitation to build a life outside of Sharpsburg. I toured the ten-mile campus with trepidation. It felt like home was a continent away. After dreaming of freedom and city life, I declined. I opted to apply to a local college near the mountains, where my friend Rachael and I could be roommates. When we visited, there were recycling bins and a large, shared green space with students strewn out studying and playing guitars. It felt manageable and idyllic in its practicality. The entire school was held within a half-mile radius, inhibiting my proneness to wander and get lost. I imagined myself there, close enough to home to feel safe but far enough away to believe I could become someone alone.

    When I decided to stay with Jake and try a long-distance

relationship, the guilt of my decision to take a break from the relationship led me to strive to let him know how much I wanted to be married. My desire for purity turned into a wild obsession to get married quickly. We tossed our caps in the air at graduation and packed Jake's car for the seven-hour drive to his new apartment across state lines.

"I just don't know how I can live without you here with me," I cried. "I know you must go, and I want the best for you. I'm sorry. I know I haven't always been the best girlfriend. I've made mistakes. But I love you."

"It's only a two-year music program. I'll move back when I finish, and we can get married while you finish your last year of college. I promise. We've been together for three years. What's two more?" His optimism was weighed down by my fear.

With a promise that we would see one another on weekends and breaks, he kissed me again on my salt-covered lips, opened the car door, and waved goodbye from out the window.

When Rachael and I arrived at our new home, we were wild with dreams. We met our two other roommates, Katie and Anne, and unpacked our boxes from the car. I enrolled in journalism classes, planning to take every writing course I could. Mid-semester, I was walking through the green space of campus when a burning conviction to pursue opening a coffee shop arose within me. I stopped and sat on the grass, retrieving my journal and pen from my backpack. I filled the pages with mission statements, drawings, hopes, and dreams. When my trance-like state subsided, and I was out of words, I stood and walked toward the admissions office to change my courses from writing to business.

Rachael invited me to join Katie and Anne for a Bible study, and I declined, staying in my room to plan out the next three years of classes. I counted down the days until I would graduate. I detailed the fastest route to a diploma so Jake and I could be together. I dreamt of our life together in the city, me owning a coffee shop while he recorded music. We would sing together and show documentaries on the weekends. I heard the door open, and voices permeated the shared living room. When I walked to the kitchen for a glass of water, my roommates were gathered around a guy I did not know playing guitar on the couch.

Katie introduced me. "Tyler, this is Christine. She grew up in Sharpsburg."

Tyler looked up from his guitar. "Oh, I think I've been through there, briefly, on my way into the city. Katie, Anne, and I grew up together, not too far from there."

"Not much there to see," I muttered in response.

"You should come join us." Tyler's blue eyes were fixed on me.

"Sure," I replied. "I could use a break from planning." Tyler moved to the corner of the couch near the window and placed a hand on the cushion beside him. The five of us talked about the transition from high school to college. We announced our paths of becoming decent citizens or, at least, a desire to find a job after graduation. I expounded on my newfound passion for opening a coffee shop and the importance of fair trade. A musician, nurse, marketing director, social worker, and coffee shop owner in the making, we were bound by our lofty ideals. As the light waned, Katie announced she had class early the next morning.

"I'm going to get to bed. Tyler is going to sleep on the couch. That's cool with you, right?" She looked in my direction.

"Yeah, absolutely," I replied, shrugging my shoulders.

Katie, Anne, and Rachael stood to leave, so I followed their lead.

Tyler called out, "Are you leaving, too?"

"I, uh," I hesitated, "I should probably go to bed with everyone else."

"Do you have class tomorrow, too?"

"No, I actually have tomorrow off, but I . . . " I tried to determine why I could not find an excuse. I had not grown accustomed to people getting to know me without Jake present. I had no reason to leave outside of the distrust that Tyler might just be another Alex.

". . . I guess I could hang out for a little longer," I finished. I walked to the kitchen to get a glass of water, returning to sit on the furthest space of the couch. Pressing my weight into the side of the armrest, I took a deep breath, noting the undeniable gaze

Tyler held. His eyes were icy blue beneath his long blonde hair. I was suddenly unsafe with myself, and in his presence, the old fear returned that, at any moment, I could be violated. When he did not move closer, I believed he would not hurt me. I turned to the only safe thing I knew, and I began to tell Tyler about Jake.

"That's cool, but I want to hear more about you."

Tyler and I stayed up late, sharing our philosophy of social reform, music, and traveling. I told him about my upcoming trip to Guatemala to stay on a coffee farm. He looked at me with the same sideways glance Jake first had when we met, and I felt a longing ache flame like the heat of June heat on my skin. When we said goodnight, a tinge in my chest criticized me. *I have stayed awake too long with this stranger.*

The following Saturday, my roommates and I drove into the city to see Tyler's band play. He swooned heavily over acoustic guitar while singing, "I want to fall in love with a hippie chick/a girl who wants to save the world through fair-trade coffee . . . " I looked around to find Rachael, to see if she caught the lyrics, and wondering if I had been found out. When he sang, I was reminded of how far away Jake was and how lonely my days felt without him by my side. After the show, Tyler hugged his friends in the crowded room. He leaned in closely, kissed my cheek, and smiled. Whiskey and spice remained heavy on his breath. Guilt saturated my thoughts as I breathed him in slowly.

"I have a boyfriend, you know," I whispered in his ear.

"I know," he replied, coolly.

He looked at me with a smile as my chest tightened.

We stood watching the stage as the next band picked up their instruments. His arm pressed into mine. We crashed into one another as the crowd pushed in like a wave toward the stage. Tyler and I got lost in the sway, singing together loudly.

As the night lingered, Tyler asked, "So where is this boyfriend you speak of?"

"He moved to the coast. He'll be finishing school next year. We have plans to get married after he graduates." I tried to sound confident against the gnawing loneliness inside of me.

He leaned in closely, his voice outmatching the music, "He

should be here with you now."

I choked back tears and remained silent, praying for the feeling to dissolve before the lights turned on in the venue. Our group of friends thinned out when the music faded, and we walked toward the exit. Tyler grabbed my waist in the back of the line, unnoticed by others. He pulled me into his chest and said, "I'm in love with you, Christine."

"You don't even know me," I half-responded, the room disappearing.

"I love the idea of you, I mean. Not you as a person. You understand?" He looked at me intently, blue eyes flashing.

I nodded yes in the confusion, and he released me into the throng of people. Tyler jumped onto the stage to close his guitar case, and I was cast into the tide of people pulling me outside into the fresh air.

Rachael found me and grabbed my hand. "Where have you been?"

"I was held back by a bunch of people. It was so crowded in there," I halfway lied.

She looked around, noting our roommates waiting for us ahead. "Hey, Tyler's really cute."

"Yeah," I shrugged, attempting to look disinterested.

"Be careful there," she warned.

"What do you mean?" I asked, feigning ignorance.

"Jake has been gone for a while, but you can't act that way around other guys. People were watching tonight, Christine. People who also know Jake. Just be careful."

"I understand," I sobbed into my hands. "I'm sorry. I just can't shake this feeling. I want him to be here. Every time we talk, everything feels so distant. His whole life is different now, and I can only catch glimpses."

Rachael put her arm around me, and we walked to the car, sitting in the backseat together. She reassured me that time would pass quickly, but I failed to recognize her truth.

"You've got to get out and start doing more," Rachael encouraged me.

In the weeks ahead, I left the temptation of Tyler behind, not answering his calls. I joined Rachael for parties, tasting alcohol for the first time and dancing long into the night. Rachael studied to become a social worker, and I listened to lectures on social justice alongside her. She delved into any organization bleeding to help others, and I rode her coattails. We slept outside and picketed injustice as though our voices would mark history. Finally, outside of our small town, Rachael and I felt brave with the opportunity. The religion of hospitality in the rural south was replaced with bold outcries from the capitol building against child slavery and economically irresponsible coffee farming. The pain of adolescence became buried in the sands of global distress, and I believed the lie that my pain was vanquished.

Each day felt like a clock stuck ticking on the same number. Obsessively attempting to capture the details of Jake's new life, I mailed him cards, set up video calls, and texted him, trying to find a way to stay connected.

I met a boy from out of town who looked at me as though he could read my soul. I drowned under the weight of his story, his loss, and his search for life. He told me I reminded him of his Mom. She had been dead for months, and I wept with him, wanting to dry up his tears by releasing my eyes to him. He held me like he wanted to remain for a lifetime. I didn't stop him. I felt more in the connection than I had wanted to feel. I indulged in the lie, hating myself more with each passing day. I wanted to be saved from myself, from this feeling of being alone. When he kissed me, I knew it was the beginning of the end with Jake.

That night, I emptied my coin jar and traveled to the ocean, arriving just in time for sunrise. I sat on the sand and watched the pull of the waves detail the very nature of my relationship with Jake. After four years, our identities were so entrenched that the slightest tug tore at the seam of the fabric we had sewn for ourselves. We had grown too heavy for these old wineskins to hold the new substance of our grown-up lives. Jake listened sullenly as I made my confession. "I'm so sorry. I don't know why I gave in. I never meant to hurt you, but I kissed him back. I feel so lonely when you aren't with me. I just . . . I just don't know how to live without you. I want to be married now. Then, all of this wouldn't exist." I placed my head onto his chest, and he pushed the hair from my eyes, "I forgive you, Christine. I know it isn't easy to be this far away from each other, but what you did hurt me. I'm going to need some time to think things through." My body was numb under the weight of Jake's arms. I was determined to forge my way through this mess I made, wading through the fear my isolation had caused. As I planned the seven-hour drive back to Atlanta the next morning, Jake said he would stay with me. He kissed my forehead as I got into the car, and he already felt like he was a continent away.

The next weekend, I arrived at the airport, hoping for some time to rebuild Jake's confidence in our relationship. He walked around to open the passenger door for me to get inside. I slid into the seat and tossed my bag into the back. I situated myself and took a deep breath. Glancing down, I noticed a torn piece of paper on the console. I picked it up and read.

Kate,
I snuck into your room tonight to say goodbye, but you were already sleeping.
Love you,
Jake

I placed it back on the console, quickly, before Jake slid into the driver's seat. He saw the paper, quickly crumpled it, and threw it onto his floorboard. With a forceful smile, Jake leaned over and kissed me on the cheek. I was numb from guilt and years of being transient, finding ways to fill in the emotional highs of others. Our lives, hidden from each other, were drifting somewhere out at sea, and there were no more lifeboats to carry us home. I didn't tell Jake I had already read the note. We made the most of our time together, but the unspoken words between us resounded loudly through our emotionally distant interactions. Jake introduced me to his new friends who play in bands and make movies. I felt small in a crowd of people who seemed to have it all—talent, beauty, and community. At a show, a skinny guy with dark hair and ripped jeans handed Jake a red solo cup. Jake looked my way before shrugging his shoulders and taking a drink.

"When did you start drinking?" I asked after the band finished.

"It's not something I do always," he responded.

"That's fine. I just thought you would have told me," my voice trailed off, thinking about the betrayal I had made by kissing someone else.

"I get it. You don't owe me an explanation. I just wish we could be open. I don't want to hide things from each other," I sighed.

Jake and I met in our small town for Thanksgiving. We strolled through the grass of the library park, where we made our promises of purity and commitment years before. My naturally long brown hair was cut short and dyed platinum blonde. I was working with a friend as his hair model. Each new style allowed me to mask my true identity or wear someone else's. I pulled an oversized fur coat over my head to hide the new person I was trying to become, attempting to remember who I was when Jake and I were still young. In this place, time rewinds. I was reminded of the girl who desired to be good, to love purely, and to be married to someone who could carry the weight of my heavy heart. Tears fell as we passionately kissed; both of us realized we had lost faith in the arms of our love.

I whispered slowly, "There must be something bigger than ourselves, or we will fall forever. Without you, I don't know who I am, and I need to figure it out. I don't want to hurt you anymore, and I don't want to hurt like this anymore."

I stared out at the ripples of the water on the lake, wondering if Fitzgerald was onto something. *Maybe we are just "boats against the current, borne back ceaselessly into the past."*[2]

When our relationship ended, I was no longer human. I sat alone on the bathroom floor of my apartment, gasping for air. For months, I struggled to find words, eat, sleep, and breathe. I was a little girl again, hiding beneath my sheets. The hollow shell of what was left became tossed into the wind. The chaff blew away, and I was left holding only a bit of straw to build back this weak foundation.

Chapter 5

Face down and headphones plugged in my ears, I shuffled across campus back to the apartment. The open green space, once so enticing, now lay desolate as the colder weather set in. My hands showed signs of poor circulation, turning white at the tips of each finger. I rubbed them together in an attempt to regain feeling, blowing warm air into balled-up fists. A flock of geese flew in a crooked V formation overhead. Two geese walked aimlessly around the middle of the grass as the others passed as if the prospect of a home was no longer appealing. I recalled a children's story that details the life of geese. When one is hurt and tired, no longer able to fly, another goose will leave the formation to stay with the healing bird until its strength returns, and they can rejoin the group. Just as the Spirit descended on Jesus after His baptism, speaking the words over Him, "This is my Son, whom I love; with him, I am well pleased," I felt a Presence of comfort knowing I was not alone.[3] Sometimes God shows up as a wild goose. My mouth involuntarily formed an awkward smile as I walked the remainder of campus, feeling slightly lighter.

When I opened the door to my bedroom, an ocean of multi-colored balloons greeted me. A large, handwritten poster served as a reminder it was my birthday. Rachael had made it her part-time job to remind me I was still alive. A card lay on the bed with a note: *You are so loved.* The balloons bounced around on the floor and knocked into the walls as I parted the helium sea with my steps. I smiled as I sat on the edge of my red comforter, staring out over the waves of balloons. *Rachael is a good friend. Good friends are hard to find.*

Over the winter months and into spring, we forged our

friendship through the onset of depression and suicidal ideation that returned in dreams. Rachael pulled me out of bed and forced me into the shower. She left cards underneath my door covered with the fresh ink of encouraging words and verses from Scripture. We stayed up late into the night, crying and laughing, eating chocolate Teddy Grahams out of the box, and stuffing our cheeks with marshmallows.

Slowly, the dream of owning a coffee shop reawakened. Rachael purchased me a new journal, and I began jotting down mission statements and slogans. The interior walls became alive as I sketched out mismatched mugs neatly hung in rows and detailed the layout of the espresso bar. We drove to the city and sipped on lattes, thinking up ways to promote future social justice movements at my apparition of a coffee shop. I absorbed the details of each space we visited, pulling out my journal to record color patterns and tasting notes.

While I worked at our local café, regulars looking for their next fix stopped by, seeking conversation. They indulged my future plans and added their own renditions of the perfect coffee shop. One day, a woman walked into the shop, eyes downcast, and fumbled to order a medium double-shot white mocha. She stared at the counter between us and extended her credit card in my general direction.

"Are you okay?" I asked quietly.

She looked up, embarrassed, as tears tumbled onto the counter. "I'm sorry." She shook her head slowly back and forth.

"I'm just having a bad day."

"Don't be sorry," I encouraged. "We all have those."

"My Mom is sick," she blurted out, barely able to finish her sentence without choking on the words.

I caught a glimpse of her necklace, a small silver cross worn daintily around her thick, milky white neck. I avoided the nudge in my spirit and the same tightness in my chest I had experienced sitting in the counselor's office years before. Walking toward the espresso machine, I grabbed a cup and pumped white chocolate into the bottom before pulling a double shot of coffee.

The routine was familiar, my hands glided through the process without thought or intention. When I set her drink on the bar, I felt the pull in my chest again. Trying to crane my neck to stretch it out, I looked around the store, ensuring no one else was in earshot. Finally, I gave into the hunch and asked quietly, "Can I . . . pray . . . for you?"

Her eyes opened wide like a surprised deer caught in the basement of my childhood house.

"I'd like that," she responded meekly.

I walked around the counter, wiping my hands on my apron. Her large frame tumbled halfway off the chair as I took a seat, stretching out my hand and placing it on top of hers where it rested on the table. *I have nothing to offer.* With that same thought, my mouth opened, and a prayer fell from my lips, unrehearsed. The woman's head dropped down to her chest, shoulders trembling as she sobbed. In a whisper, I extended an amen and held her hands as she cried. She looked up and silently offered a *thank you*. My chest relaxed, and I smiled knowingly.

"There is a purpose, somewhere, hidden in our pain," I waxed poetic. Finding words felt like translating a second language, yet minutes prior, prayer had come so naturally, "You just have to look for it."

She nodded her head, wiping away tears. Her thin pink lips turned upward, resembling a smile. "Thank you."

We stood from the table, and she embraced me. Without another word, she picked up her paper cup and walked through the door. The bell dinged behind her, and I exhaled peacefully. Where passion and pain intersected, I found purpose. I strengthened the legs underneath me by accepting many more gentle invitations to trust my intuition. I found faith, despite failure, by risking vulnerability. I began slowing down to talk with cashiers at the checkout line or smiling when passing by strangers. Sometimes, people stopped to have deep, meaningful conversations. Other times, interactions were not quite as pleasant, like the time I gave a package of crackers to a homeless woman and they were thrown back in my face or the confessions from those who had undergone abortions and lived in secret shame. With every story, intimacy was found in the connection with sharing. With each step forward, I found my humanity wrapped up in the relationships with those around me. Jake remained my hope for a future husband, but with each invitation of the Spirit to move closer to others, my heart grew in its capacity for greater love.

Preparing for the last few semesters of college, Rachael spent time reading news of child soldiers in Africa. The world was breaking around her, and she could not hold all of the pieces together. She wasted the next three weeks lying in bed, missing classes, and reading mail from social justice organizations. As the holidays crept in, she was divided between the plans of her divorced parents. No longer a child, she had to decide. I indulged her by watching the same movie on repeat about a couple walking through divorce that ended up staying together at the very end. Her fear was tangible.

"What if this is the story of my life?" she asked as the credits rolled.

My family and I have had little contact since I started college. April was busy finishing the requirements for her chiropractic license, while Mom and Michelle took turns staying home with Braxton. On the occasions we spoke, I felt less known and less attached. My foundations, log cabin home and childhood church were crumbling beneath me.

I sat beside Rachael on her bed. After a quiet pause, I confessed, "I don't know, Rachael. At least there's a happy ending in this one. I keep thinking Jake will walk through the door and tell me everything will be okay. After being together for four years, I thought we'd be planning our wedding this year." My voice trailed off as I sank into the memory of us lying together on the picnic blanket underneath the big oak tree. I stared down at my hand, my fingers stark naked without my ring.

"Christine, there's someone else out there for you. I know you loved Jake, but it's over, and you're better for it. He's not coming back." She studied my face, but I did not look at her for fear of losing self-control.

"I know." I gave in to emotion. I whispered through tears, "I just miss him. And I know it's a terrible time to talk about this with you, but Mom called yesterday. April is getting divorced."

"What? Didn't she just get married a couple of months ago?" Rachael asked.

"Yeah, I know. Mom didn't give any details. She even sounded like she was considering it for herself, like it was a good idea. It was very strange. I don't know what to think about marriage anymore. No one seems to stay together. In the end, everyone leaves." The words lingered. It became my truth.

In the silence that followed, we realized there was no consolation for either of us. We sat and watched a dark screen, scrolling the names of those who will never be properly appreciated—the onsite catering company, gaffer, and third production cameraman. The same refrain repeated as the movie's soundtrack became a scroll of my memories with Jake. The pain was overwhelming. "I don't have any answers except that there is a promise that true love never fails. I want to believe that is true. I want to believe there is a God, bigger than our current circumstances, that works all things for our good. I want a therapeutic hippie Jesus, but I can't find him in Scripture." I laid back in bed and turned toward Rachael, "We're not in Kansas anymore, and when we wake up, I fear there is no home that either of us will be welcomed back into. This growing-up business is harder than anyone told me."

As I left for class the next morning, I noticed Rachael was still in bed.

I shook her. "You've got to go to class eventually, Rachael. Staying in bed will not change the world's state." She grunted and rolled over, her back to me. I sighed, giving up, and closed the door quietly behind me as I left for finals.

Come spring, Rachael failed her classes, packed her things from our apartment, and moved back home. "It's just for the summer." Rachael's voice sounded optimistic on the phone.

I explored my next steps of adulthood, making a plan with her. "I only have two classes left that I'll finish this summer, and I'm looking to move into the lofts downtown. What do you think? You can come to live with me in August and finish your classes. It's close enough to campus."

"Yes!" Rachael screamed into the receiver. "That is perfect!"

Rachael found a job at a pizza place over the summer, close to her mom's house where we grew up. I continued working overtime at the café to save money for the future coffee shop and our new apartment. In July, I put the down payment on the apartment for us and began to pack my belongings to move from the apartments on campus to my first grown-up space. Graduation came and went. It was a lonely time without Rachael or Jake there to celebrate alongside me, so I opted out of walking with my classmates. Instead, I drove back to my hometown to meet with Rachael and talk about our future together. We met at a coffee shop, where she rushed toward me, hugging me tightly when I walked through the door.

"Hey, I've missed you!" I said into her shoulder. Rachael was a head taller than me. When she looked down in my direction, her large blue eyes were outlined with black liner. Her once naturally light brown hair was dyed dark, with bangs draped across her forehead. She smelled thickly of jasmine and amber.

"I've missed you, too!" she squealed in a high-pitched tone I didn't recognize. "How are you?" she asked as we found a place in line for coffee.

"I'm doing well. New look, I see. I like it!" I declared, gesturing toward her hair.

"Yeah, it's been so fun working at the pizza shop. You would never even know it's the same town we grew up in. Everyone downtown is cool, and there's a new bar next door that I'm looking to get a job at for an extra shift or two. Since Jake and I started working . . . " Her voice trailed off to a dead end.

"Jake?" I asked, confused.

"Yeah, sorry, I thought maybe you already knew," she continued deliberately.

The barista's voice barked from behind the machine, "What are you drinking today?"

"Oh, um. Sorry, hold on." I stared at the menu board. The letters blurred together, and I was grateful I knew my order without reading it. "I'll have an iced latte, please," I said methodically. I paid the cashier and waited silently at the counter for my drink to be prepared. When it arrived, I followed Rachael to an open table and sat across from her.

"So, you're working with Jake?" I interrogated further.

"Yeah, he moved back a few months ago. His parents bought him a house with his friend, Nathan. You remember his roommate from college?" she inquired as if I had not taken the seven-hour drive to stay with them countless times.

"Oh," my voice was flat. "Cool." I tried to play off the pain in my stomach; the sense of betrayal rose toward my throat. I diverted the subject sharply, "So, you've looked into your classes for next month, right? The deadline is in a week."

"A little bit. What about you? How are your plans for the coffee shop?" She returned the question to me, unconsciously avoiding the inevitable.

"I'm working on the last few pages of my business proposal to take to the city to get my license for the coffee shop. We can move into the apartment in two weeks. I put the final payment down for our place yesterday. When are you planning on coming up?" I asked, hopeful to leave this town I had worked so hard to escape.

Rachael looked down at her cup and pressed her lips together. I continued staring at her, waiting anxiously for the response.

When nothing came, I urged, "What's going on?"

"I'm sorry, Christine." Rachael's ocean eyes filled with tears. "I just can't make it work," she continued. "My parents won't pay for college after what happened, and I'm just not making enough money to be able to pay for the loft."
I swallowed hard, feeling confused.

"Why didn't you tell me, Rachael?" My desire for empathy shifted into quiet despair.

"I'm sorry. I don't know what else to say." The tears spilled over onto the napkin sitting on the table between us.

"I'm sorry, too." I finally regulated my breathing, shoving the anger back down into the pit of my belly. "I just . . . I just don't have anyone else. I also can't get out of the contract I already signed for us," I said, reality settling in.

"I know. I'm really sorry, Christine. This will be hard, but we'll still see each other. And I'll come up to visit." She paused. "There's one more thing I need to tell you just because I don't want you to hear it from someone else."

"Okay?" I hesitated.

"I've been hanging out with Jake and Nathan a lot since Jake moved back home," she stated in a pseudo-confession. "Jake asked that you not come over when we're hanging out. He said it would just be too painful for him. I know you'll understand."

My chest expanded. I wanted to reach for her hand, to pray this new reality away. I wanted to slap Jake's name from her lips to let her know how much it hurt me to hear it spoken, to remember all of the times she had told me to forget about him, to let him go, to push him away. Now, sitting across from her, I was painfully aware she had chosen a friendship with him instead of a future with me. All words were swallowed up, and I wanted to flip the table, to yell, "Traitor!" My teeth were clenched as I turned toward the door. I was suddenly very tired, and no amount of caffeine will suffice.

"I have to go," I sighed. "I love you. I just have to figure out some things. Like what I'm going to do with this loft, I guess." Feeling left my body as the ghost of me floated up from the table and drifted out the door. I cried the entire drive to an empty apartment, feeling angry and betrayed.

Michelle offered to move in with me, and we made space in the laundry closet for Braxton to have his own room. In the two years after graduation, I wandered. A new acquaintance met me for coffee. Boisterous in laughter and life, she removed her shoe to show me her freshly inked foot: *Not all who wander are lost.*[4] While working at the coffee shop, I found temporary connections with cocaine dealers, hippies, fire breathers, racist Republicans, and abortion-advocating Democrats. So as not to reveal the emptiness of my existence, I wanted to bottle up their experiences and live life wildly through them. I spent weekends with Michelle, dancing in crowded rooms filled with people. I listened to their stories, feeling the ache of the human condition and the fear of leading a meaningless existence. We danced and drank. Every man hoped to fill his loneliness with the loveliness of a woman, and every woman hoped to feel lovely by not being alone. I learned the rhythm of conformity without denying the moralistic standard blazed around my ring finger. Even without my ring, the desire for purity and intimacy resonated deeply in my belief that there was a person who could love me unconditionally. I remained untainted by the lie of temporary intimacy as I listened to stories of men and women who left each other's beds emptier than when they had entered them. These stories fueled my craving for deep, meaningful relationships. I walked through pews and danced in the clubs; neither revealed a capacity for the authenticity I desired. Distracting myself into exhaustion, I evaded sleep and fell into my sheets alone. *God, there has to be more to life than this.*

     Michelle met a bartender who moved in with the three of us. Our space grew a little tighter as their relationship developed and marriage became the forefront of the conversation. A girl whom I worked with at the café offered me a room in her house. Alissa taught me to read tarot cards and claimed to understand the hidden meaning of our lives according to the stars. She analyzed my dreams and encouraged me to think beyond the terms of my hand-me-down religion. We drank raspberry beer on her back porch and watched the weeping willows sway in the breeze. On the weekends, we would scrounge up our money from working at the coffee shop to buy skeins of yarn to make scarves and canvases to paint. We made our way through hiking trails, naming each one. She claimed fairies lived amidst the flowers and colors emitted from the trees. We stared at the town below and caught the light refracting from the structures. I enjoyed listening to her vantage point and imagined a world where pain could be summed up by simply letting go. When it was quiet, my brain rattled with untold stories. My body bore the marks of unspoken pain. Letting go was bound up in forgiveness, but I could not find the path to begin. I talked a lot about Jesus when I drank, and Alissa's friends began calling me "church mouse," even though I had not stepped near a church for some time.

Jake and I were at church five days a week in high school, writing songs and practicing with the band. It was safe, and it was good. Church had become a foreign territory, but I often thought of when God called my name. I wanted to believe Jesus was who he claimed to be in scripture, but when I looked around at those who called themselves Christian, I could not see the evidence of Christ in their lives. With one breath, they sang on Sundays, and in the next, they spoke hateful words. So, I kept talking about Jesus in hopes He would show up again outside of a church building like God did that day in my bedroom.

I smoked cigarettes to remind myself to breathe. Alissa said she was going to quit and begin doing yoga. I told her I would do yoga, but I'd probably still smoke when I drank. She laughed at me and said that was fine; there were no rules other than the ones we made. There was an old VCR in the living room, and we moved the coffee table aside in the mornings. The recording of Steve Ross was outdated, and Alissa fast-forwarded through the commercial breaks. My breathing was heavy, but my body felt light. I moved and contorted into the positions instructed, glancing over at Alissa as we tried not to fall. Alissa and I laughed through the first three weeks of our new practice. Gradually, I started finding grace in the movements. My body strengthened, and my breathing slowed. We lay on the floor at the end of our session in savasana, corpse pose. *This may be the end of my life, and I have nothing to show for it.* My chest rose and fell slowly as I lay on the rug next to Alissa. My palms were open to receive. I breathed. *In and out. In and out.*

Alissa talked about seeing white elephants and colors popping from people's heads around her. I saw Jesus. He was just there, hands outstretched, waiting. There were no elephants, no colors, just Him. I wept, lying on my back in the living room. There was so much time wasted thinking about all the people who had left and all the things I had done and left undone. It was time to begin again. It's time to begin breathing again. It was time to stop smoking and start trusting Jesus wanted more for me than I could ever want for myself. In my imagination, I released Jake into His care. I imagined taking each memory like a polaroid, clipping it onto a laundry line, and watching them float by in a gentle breeze as they passed. I released myself from the guilt and shame, for all I had done outside of love. I tried hard to follow the rules but could not keep up. I wanted nothing but to be good. To be loveable. To be loved purely. I tried, and I failed. My kingdom had come to its end. Everything would have to start anew.

Derek entered the coffee shop. His eyes curved in deep rainbow shapes, resembling a bloodhound. His full lips, slightly pursed, sat pronounced on a narrow face. Derek was short in stature with a receding hairline that he shaved close to the sides. He wore a trucker hat, tight jeans, cowboy boots, and a shirt that acted as a billboard, displaying an obscure band name across the front. I stood behind the counter, intrigued.

Alissa elbowed me in the side. "I think you two would have a lot to talk about." I was immediately uneasy. Derek and I glanced at one another with quick judgment, understanding the tone behind the comment. We disregarded the weight of assumption as we gained momentum from the chatter. We exchanged hellos, and after serving him a black coffee, we drifted back into our previous conversations. Due to small-town living, Derek and I naturally began seeing more of one another, and in time, we realized the spark of similar interests. We discussed the Old Testament and the need for grace. Both of us acknowledged our unwillingness to be bound by the confines of a church organization. We laughed about smoking while doing yoga and found our communion within craft beer and independent films. Derek and I were charged with our passions. We could both argue about theology, art, music, and literature. He ignited creativity in me that had lain dormant since Jake and I walked away from one another. I began writing again in snippets, ornamenting coffee shop napkins with wandering thoughts.

In high school, I aptly labeled myself as "the dumb kid in all of the smart kid classes." One day, a friend told me, in confidence, that he liked Jake, but I would never be satisfied by Jake's intellect. I disregarded this notion by dismissing my own ravenous curiosity to be socially accepted. Late-night talks with Derek made me realize some boys thirsted for deeper knowledge, weighted emotions, and the capacity to counter my desire to be right. I could also keep up with Derek's intellectual race and challenged his pretension in a way that made me feel like an equal. In this space, I no longer had to hide under my femininity or become submissive to the male standard of superiority. It was not only welcomed, but it was encouraged.

Derek and I sat in the dark, movie credits rolling, lost in another conversation. When we finally noticed, he stood and turned off the television. "You have to listen to this new album. But you have to listen to it all the way through. You can stay," Derek stated without a question.

"Sure," I responded with a casual shrug of my shoulders. We lay on the floor of his tiny apartment, eyes closed, immersed in the new record. The carpet was imprinted by our silhouettes. I sank deeper into the experience of each melody, taking myself away from the pain that slowly pulsed to the surface when I was still with my thoughts. Two large trunks sat beside the island in the living room like discarded pirate treasure. They were filled with pure gold, hundreds of CDs, and music I had never heard. The trunks were the only pieces of furniture to decorate the scene, save a large exercise bench that served as a poor substitute for a couch. A sense of satisfaction crept in as the album ended. We sat up to continue discussing societal norms and collective unconsciousness before he pressed me on my last relationship. My vulnerability bridged a gap of connection between us. I shared with painful detail, opening up wounds of the past. Derek nodded in understanding, his eyes two mirrors staring back at me.

Like a virus, the attention spread through my body, and I allowed it to seep into my skin. Desires reawakened, the gnawing ache of being known and loved. Desire became displaced, a refugee within the walls of Derek's apartment. I apologetically let the tears come in mighty waves, raising my chest in great heaves. Derek remained still. He did not offer a comforting arm or chest. I wanted to be held, to be told this would pass. I would eventually learn to unlove Jake, and the pain will dissolve.

Derek stated matter-of-factly, "You simply learn to live in the darkness until it becomes light."

"What if it never becomes light?" I asked, drying my tears

with the back of my hand.

"Then you learn to love sadness," He laughed. "It can make for some great art."

I was embarrassed as the saltwater pooled around our bodies. I stood to leave, feeling my head pounding from the hangover of vulnerability.

Nights later, the credits rolled from an expired film, and again, Derek and I found ourselves the last two people in the room. Derek leaned in close and kissed me.

I pushed him away, "You can't kiss me. I don't love you."

He laughed assuredly and, with an apt superiority, stated, "That doesn't matter. You're my girlfriend now. So, that makes it alright."

I was stunned by the confidence in his voice. The rebel in me was silenced, and I complied. I was too far out of reach to find myself worthy of anything better. The only real relationship I had ever known had been drowned by the sea. The last shred of will I held was abdicated to a man I barely knew. Somehow, though, I was convinced I would no longer suffer, feeling inadequate and alone. I hid behind Derek, believing he would lead me to a new beginning where I could let go of any possibility of marrying Jake.

The flicker of my phone screen revealed Rachael's name. I quickly pressed the silence button to ignore the call. Seeing her name surfaced the anger of her choice to betray me, her choice to leave me alone, to sort out life apart from those I loved the most. I wondered what Jake was doing, if he had a new girlfriend, but mostly, I wondered if he was happier without me. I walked to the refrigerator to see what was inside. A cucumber. A bottle of vodka. One jug of milk. Opening the cabinet, I retrieved a glass and poured out a swig of vodka, adding a splash of milk and some coffee liquor. Derek turned on a record as we stood in silence. I pushed back the tears that were appearing and took a sip of my drink.

"Be careful," Derek stated. "You wouldn't want to get any bigger than you are now, would you? And anyway, you'll have to stay here since you started drinking that."

"It's just a drink," I responded.

"Yeah, tell that to the cop that pulls you over," Derek stated as he walked toward his bedroom. "You can sleep on the floor. I have extra blankets."

I finished off the contents of my glass and walked to the bathroom, spreading a line of toothpaste across my finger. Staring in the mirror, I pretended to brush my teeth, but I did not recognize my own face. The blonde had begun to strip from my roots, and dark circles were underneath my eyes. *Maybe he is right. Maybe I do need to start watching my weight again.*

Derek and I wasted our days drinking, painting, listening to music, and frequenting pool halls. He ordered a light beer for me, and I choked it down. Our once mutual conversations slowly became an empty space, existing within the same place as we both worked out our creative interests. I brought my camera and journal everywhere we went to document life from a different perspective, trying out what a relationship felt like with someone who was not Jake.

"Your hair is getting longer. I really like it short," Derek said over sushi.

"I like my hair longer. I'm growing it out," I responded, pushing the chopsticks around my plate.

"Oh, I guess if that's what you want to do. I just thought you wanted to be attractive," he said without looking up.

"I do want to be attractive; that's why I am growing my hair out," I repeated.

"Hm." Derek set down his chopsticks and looked at me, "Are you going to eat all of that?"

"I plan on it, why?" I asked.

"I just thought I would eat whatever you didn't want," he said, picking back up where he had left off on his plate.

My stomach flipped, and I laid down my chopsticks, pushing the plate toward him.

"Hey, thanks," Derek smiled as he finished off both of our meals and paid the bill.

I sat in silence, considering the times I had vacillated between eating too much and far too little, never allowing my body to determine the boundaries of nourishment.

The following week, I cut my hair short.

"You look amazing!" Derek said as I entered his apartment before going to a show. "Wait, here. I made something for you."

He pulled a pair of shoes from his closet and took them into the kitchen, leaving me to switch out my old self for the newer version, which looked much more like him. He presented me with freshly painted shoes with an awkward monster-like creature brushed onto both sides.

"There, now we can actually go out," Derek noted as he looked at my newly purchased skinny jeans and a t-shirt he pulled out of his dresser for me to wear.

"Umm . . . thanks," I responded, bending down to remove my sandals and squeeze my toes into the shoes.

"You don't want to look fat, do you?" he asked, without expecting an answer.

"What is that supposed to mean?" I clearly did not meet his expectations.

"You know what I mean! It's not just you; it's your clothes. You should be glad you can do something about it if you want to. How do you think I feel? I have already started losing my hair. Do you think I like shaving my head?"

My heart was beating fast. "I know that's not your fault, Derek. No one has ever said anything about your hair, though."

"You have no idea how hard it is. All you have to do is work out more, and you won't even have a problem. I can't do anything about mine." He grabbed the keys and walked toward the door. "You wearing those other clothes makes you look even bigger than you are. That's all I'm saying. I'm not a big guy, Christine. Have you ever thought about my perspective? No guy wants to be with a girl who is bigger than him. I'm just trying to help you," Derek continued his mental tangent aloud.

Tears burned hot behind my eyes, "Maybe you should just go by yourself."

He turned around fast. "I'm not going by myself, Christine. You're coming. What would you want me to tell everyone?"

I held a deep breath inside my chest, hoping it would stop the tears from falling.

"You're right. I'm sorry. I know I could work out more often. It's just been hard lately," I said quietly.

"Excuses are for weak people. Besides, I have a workout bench in my living room. You have no excuse," Derek walked out the door, leaving it ajar.

I stood for a minute, surveying the space, feeling confused by the conversation. *How did I end up apologizing?*

Derek had taken the blank canvas of a person I existed in and turned it into his newest project. The Truth within me—any remnant of joy or will—was exchanged for acceptance. I simply desired to feel loved again, even if that love was a poor counterfeit substitute. It came with an unforeseen cost. Derek's words slowly began to dictate what clothes were acceptable, which music held substance, and how books were tolerable, only if disregarded by others. Our small group of friends slowly dissipated, some moving out of state. For the others, Derek declared each had a tragic flaw that was no longer worthy of his attention or affection. As such, I should not hang out with them anymore, either. His air of pretension, coupled with my insecurity, held us on a tightrope. I wanted to jump off, but the fear of falling kept me on my tiptoes. Already empty, it was easy to fill me with all of the fantastical ideals Derek wanted from a woman.

When Derek announced he was taking a trip to Germany for two weeks, I exhaled a sigh of relief. He asked if I would stay in his apartment while he was gone. Naturally, as an introvert, it was a welcome reprieve. Determined to find common ground and an interest of my own, I embarked on a mission to spend the next two weeks listening to over 200 bands. I spent my days, eyes closed, worshiping each note or wincing at those not in sync with my interest. I kept a journal detailing the ones I liked most to discuss with Derek when he arrived back in the States. Each day he was gone, Derek wrote to tell me about the places he explored, people he met, and historical monuments he wanted us to see together one day. On the day before he arrived home, I opened my inbox and read:

Christine,
My time in Germany has come to an end. There's so much I saw and learned here. If it has taught me anything, I don't want to be alone. Let's get married when I get back. You'll have to meet my parents. They will love you.
Derek

I looked around the apartment and wondered what it would look like to build a life there together, as if I had another choice. The hope of a life with Jake faded to a blank space in my memory. The workout bench stared back at me. I did not respond to the email.

Derek's Mom lived in a rural town where feed & seed stores could be found on any corner. I entered the smoky apartment, and she greeted me with a welcoming hug. Her face shape and height resembled Derek's, but her lips were thin outlines of a smile. She walked over to Derek and kissed him on the mouth. Watching a mother kiss her twenty-year-old son so intently took me aback, but I dismissed the judgment, having never been a mom. As we walked toward the dining room to sit down, a lingerie magazine sat open on the table. She excitedly picked it up and scanned a few pages back to reveal a lacy red piece she announced she had just purchased for her fourth husband. I looked to Derek for confirmation that this was not a normal conversation when you first meet someone, nor a conversation you should have with your mom.

Instead, Derek laughed, "Good choice, Mom."

I sat uncomfortably for the next half hour until Derek's new stepdad arrived. The four of us made our way to a dark pool hall filled with men with mustaches and women in tight jeans, bangs as high as the ceiling. Derek ordered me a light beer. He commented on how good his Mom looked while looking down at the skirt I chose to wear to meet his family. I inhaled my anger into my chest, where it sank low into my belly, and forced a smile. Then, I slammed the cue ball hard with my pool stick and ordered another beer to celebrate my victorious shot.

On the ride home, Derek told me his Mom liked me a lot before holding out a small box.

"What is that?" I asked.

Derek dropped the box onto my lap. I picked it up and opened it slowly. The box contained three dead marriages, three broken vows, and three unwedded rings.

"You can pick whichever one you want. I don't care," Derek slurred.

"Oh, wow. That feels special," I responded flatly.

"You're so ungrateful. What's your problem? Just pick a ring. Isn't this what you want? To be married?" His voice grew louder, but his eyes never left the road.

"I don't want to feel how you make me feel," I said. The anger was tangible.

"All I have ever done is love you. I am giving you a ring! What else do you want?"

"I'm still in love with Jake! I have been since we met," the words spilled out, filling the car with their weight.

"Give it up, Christine. He doesn't want you." Derek turned his gaze toward me briefly, wanting to see my reaction.

I stared at the rings, hoping they would change me somehow and bring clarity. I had read the Scriptures. I wanted selfless love. A love that served, comforted, basked in each others' light, and held space for growth. I wanted a walk to the aisle filled with joyful excitement, with friends and family cheering us on. When I thought about a wedding with Derek, the chairs were empty. With Rachael gone and not feeling welcome in my hometown, shame had pushed me onto an island of my own making. I shut the lid. We would have to elope.

We drove the rest of the way home in silence, unable to acknowledge the underlying sway of emotion underneath the anger and fear. I walked into the apartment, making my way to the bathroom. I locked the door behind me, turning on the fan to cry alone, unheard. It was a ritual cleansing. When I emerged, Derek was in the living room painting. He did not look up.

"You can meet my dad next week," Derek stated.

"Why would I do that?" I swallowed hard.

"He'll want to have made his opinion about you before I tell him we're getting married," Derek said, dipping his brush into a deep red.

"Great," I responded flatly. I continued to walk toward the door to leave when he said, "He found his wife online in Japan. She doesn't speak English."

"Brilliant," I muttered to myself. "It's all starting to make sense."

Once a new pair of shoes has run through the mud, they

no longer carry the same luster. And so, in the brief time of our relationship, we hit a space of self-awareness in which Derek's truest self surfaced. Porn replaced intimacy; eruptions of anger began to bubble under the surface. For a while, I could take the pot off of the stovetop quickly enough to prevent anything from boiling over. The once-intellectual conversations became deriding fits of misogynistic rants, leaving me feeling worthless and empty. When I chose to express emotion about his comments, he turned my feelings into a personal attack on his character. He exploded into a rage before crying on the floor about always being misunderstood. I was left to comfort him or to leave, and if I chose to leave, he told me I lacked love and empathy. The cycle of anger and self-pity dragged on for months, and Derek could no longer take a vested interest in anyone outside himself.

  This attribute became apparent when he crossed his arms over his chest and leaned back in the chair, proclaiming, "My biggest fear is to be forgotten."

  "What do you mean forgotten? The girl you dated twice will leave you and not call back?" I wondered aloud.

  "No, like forgotten. Never to be thought of again," his voice spoke confidently in his fear.

  "By whom?" I asked.

  "Anyone I meet," he stated boldly.

  "I am pretty sure there are many people who forget you daily," I was bordering on sarcasm, but his demeanor was so serious that I searched for clarity. "Are you saying you want every single person who ever meets you to remember you forever?"

  "Yes, I think they should."

  "Derek, you can't be serious. Just think about it. You go to the grocery store, and the clerk bagging your groceries is tracking the dollar amounts for each hour he has spent working. He wants to buy a twelve-pack of beer and pay the rent. That boy has already forgotten you before he has transferred grocery bags from his hand to yours," I said.

  I kept pressing and gesturing toward the waitress, "What about this girl? She has been standing around these tables for hours, asking the same questions, memorizing mediocre food items, and analyzing how the cook line is least likely to harass her. The bartender asked her out twice in the past two months, and she turned him down both times. She is trying to figure out whether or not she can still make it work with her boyfriend, who lives across the state line, and pay her way through college. You come in once and tell her which food best meets your craving. She walks to your table twice more: once to deliver your meal and the next to slap down your check. Do you think she is going to remember you?" I squinted my eyes at him and pushed my chest forward from where I sat. No response.

    I relaxed back into the chair and took a long drink of the Belgian beer I had ordered, despite Derek attempting to course-correct my order to a lighter-calorie option. There are six billion people on this planet, and I had chosen to be in a relationship with the most self-centered of them all. Derek was rigid in his chair, dark eyes fixed on my own. Apparently, staring at the person in front of you is analogous to the need to be heard, even when you have little to no merit. Here we go again. He's drunk, and I get the pleasure of listening to his endless rants while ending the night by driving us both home. Oh, joy!

    "Ok," I changed gears, "I apologize . . . Can you tell me what makes you memorable to people?"

    "Everything. It's just who I am," he smiled big. "It shouldn't need any more explanation."

    I reached before me, dragging my glass to the table's edge. I picked it up and vowed not to put it down again until I had emptied its contents. *Please, God, help me forget him.*

    At some point, unbeknownst to me, I had fallen down the rabbit hole and lost track of time. I began to awaken to the reality I had not chosen this relationship in my purest mind, nor did I want to continue in it with any ounce of sobriety. I was terrified to stay but even more so to leave. I was my Dad's daughter, no longer able to feel the world's reality where I inactively participated. Some days, the alcohol made me laugh. Mostly, it made me numb. Feeling too overwhelmed to be interesting, I completely disengaged with the world around me. Derek's outbursts became more frequent, and I spent my days trying not to provoke him into anger. I stayed small, stayed quiet, and stayed subdued by a lack of food and greater amounts of alcohol. I was searching for myself in everything and everyone except within me.

One evening, Derek left the house with some friends, and I fell asleep on a forsaken floor mattress in his apartment. I did not hear the door open when he knelt beside me to wake me up. I sat up, screaming at his touch. I was subconsciously terrified of the life I was living with this man I did not love. I tried to calm myself, embarrassed. I laughed it off apologetically, but I could not shake the feeling.

Soon after, we spent the day with Derek's father and wife, a far cry from our experience with his mom. Derek was serious, and the conversation focused on work accolades, military stories, and educational achievements. When we arrived back at the apartment, I noted the change in tone when Derek was around his father.

"You seemed a bit on edge with your dad," I said. "I never really thought you cared about what you were discussing."

"What do you mean? Do you think you know everything about me?" He felt challenged.

I backed down, "No, that's not what I'm saying. It just felt like you were trying to prove something to him, that's all."

"You don't know anything about our relationship. How could you? You can't even keep up with your own," Derek reached into the refrigerator and grabbed a beer.

My brain raced to Jake, noting the warmth and comfort within our meager attempt at love. Then, my mind streamed from Alex to my father and any other attempt at gaining acceptance from my relationship with men. I realized I could not keep reliving the same reality with Derek, expecting things to change within him. I had to change myself, which started with leaving the environment. I believed there was something better out there than marrying a man who could not even love himself, especially since I believed the essence of God is love. These feelings took hold and strengthened my bones. I grabbed a plastic grocery bag from the cabinet and filled it with anything in the apartment that belonged to me: my camera, some CDs, and a T-shirt. I took a deep breath, bag in hand, and walked to the door. My head was up; my heart was strong.

"Derek," I choked, "there is so much potential in you if you could only use it for the good of others. You are the most self-absorbed person I have ever met, and I refuse to spend another day here. Having nowhere to go is still better than being with you." I turned to face the door, my hands trembling with fear. His left hand tightly gripped my arm while the other slapped hard against my cheek. The bag fell to the ground as I stumbled two steps backward. My mind reeled with the pain and shock. Immediately, Derek dropped to his knees and began to sob.

I was stunned.

Hot tears formed behind my eyelids. I examined the scene, somehow feeling more courageous than before.

"I won't do this anymore," I said in an eerily calm tone. I picked up the bag while I watched his body contort into a fetal position on the floor. I closed the door behind me.

I walked to the car in the stillness of night and began to drive, not knowing where to go. The ache in my jaw reduced to a warm sensation. My head pounded. My mind was set.
There had to be something better than this.

I settled into the rhythm of life again as work at the coffee shop became my only exposure to relationships outside the occasional family visit. As the milk broke through layers of espresso, I listened empathetically to each person's story. My regulars had names. They told me about their daughters' new teachers at school and their sons' baseball games. They tipped well and asked me how I was doing. I came up with short answers that appeased the nature of my work while not over-sharing. Others became reduced to a drink name. *You're the double-tall white chocolate mocha with two extra pumps, right?* I had forgotten my name, forgotten what it was to hold the Divine within my frame. I overworked to feel my worth and sank into the monotony of feeling alive.

My phone buzzed as I stood by the espresso machine. I reached into my pocket, and Derek's name flashed across the screen. After two months of silence, I was surprised by the attempt to contact me. *What could he want?* I waited to see if he left a voicemail, but nothing came through. I finished my shift and walked to my car. *Missed Call.* Hoping to receive an apology or be able to relay that I am over the thought of having a relationship with him ever again, I pressed the button to return his call. Taking a slow, deep breath as it rang, I closed the door to my car and waited.

"Hey," Derek answered.

"Hi," I responded.

"I have that room booked for the beach next week as we had planned. I wanted to know if you're still coming," his voice sounded as if he were in an open space.

"Where are you?" I asked.

"Just hanging out with a friend," he laughed.

"Yeah, I'm not sure you remember what happened when I saw you last, but no. No, I can't come with you," I shook my head, placing a hand on my cheek.

"We'll go as friends," Derek's voice on the other end of the phone was hopeful. "I just need a chance to say I'm sorry. I never meant to hurt you. Just give me the chance to make it up to you, Christine. I love you. We can go as friends. You can trust me."

I had already taken time off from my work schedule. It was only one night. I was silent for a long while.

"Fine," I finally complied. "As friends."

"As friends," he repeated.

It was a long drive to the beach. I masked hurt feelings and ill intentions with loud music and excitement to sit by the ocean. We arrived at the hotel, and Derek opened the door and put his bag on the bench beside the bed.

"There's only one bed," I noted. "I am not sleeping in the same bed as you."

Derek shrugged it off quickly, "You didn't respond to my calls, so I booked one bed thinking you weren't coming. What do you want me to do, drive you home?"

"You didn't tell me there wouldn't be separate beds. You know I am not going to sleep with you, Derek."

"You can sleep on the chair," he offered. His true colors.

"You should have let me know. I refuse to sleep in the same

bed with you."

"What do you think I am? Do you think I don't have any emotions? I love you, Christine! I am just trying to make this right!" Derek's anger escalated as he began to beat his chest.

I wanted to laugh as his behavior reminded me of the gorillas I had seen on TV. He became reduced to a caricature in my head. Wild hands flailed up to the ceiling as his body became smaller and smaller. I wanted to step on him and flatten him to the earth.

Without emotion, I responded, "You have to calm down. You are acting like a belligerent fool."

We sat in the silence of the scene for a few more seconds as Derek fumed.

"I will never be with you again, Derek," I said calmly. "You have to accept that and move on. Your anger is just like my Dad's, and I swore to myself I would never marry anyone who would act like this. I'm done. You said we could come as friends. I am going to hold you to that."

I took a deep breath and tried to control the rush of emotion, returning to why I chose to walk away. I quickly gathered a swimsuit and walked into the bathroom to change out of my dress. As it fell to the floor, I smiled. I noted that for the first time, I was not wearing hand-me-downs or clothing forced upon me by another person's opinion of what I should look like.

From behind the door, I continued, "We can figure out the bed thing later. Let's go to the beach and enjoy our time here, okay?"

"Yeah," Derek agreed. "There's no reason for you to make such a big deal about things."

I ignored his comment, grabbing a book and towel. "You can come find me when you're ready."

Walking to the beach, I noted the strength that had returned to my voice even in the past few months. Derek and I spent the day mindlessly in the sand, distracting ourselves in shops along the pier and eating at a nice restaurant. Consciously, I remained distant and answered questions without much detail. After dinner, we found a pool hall and ordered drinks.

The bartender remarked, "Must be a lucky man to find a girl like her."

I promptly responded, "Oh, we aren't together."

Derek turned to me, and I could see the anger begin to take hold. He ordered two more beers for himself and drank them back-to-back. As we played a round of pool, a few older men filtered into the dank room. Derek left the table and asked if the men wanted to join him to play another round. I took a seat on the side of the room to watch. Coming to the beach as friends turned out to be more complicated than I imagined, having brought all of the horror of Derek's features to the forefront. He did not invite me to play with them, taking the next hour to finish two more games and eight beers. I finally walked over and told him I needed to go, still trying to figure out where I would sleep. He was intoxicated, and I ducked underneath his arm to drape it around my shoulder. He steadied himself to stand.

"Where are your keys?" I asked.

"I'm not letting you drive my car," he said into the air.

"You're drunk, Derek. Give me your keys," I demanded.

"No," his gaze met mine as he shook my arm away from him. Stumbling through the door, we made our way to the gravel lot.

"I'm not getting in that car with you," he slurred.

"Fine," I said, shoving the keys into my back pocket. "We'll walk. The hotel is only a few blocks from here."

He could not form sentences as I hoisted the weight of his arm and side on my own. This time, he did not fight me.

When we finally made it back to the hotel, I unlocked the door and threw him off of me onto the bed. My shoulder ached. He was passed out when I removed his bag from the bench.

I guess I will sleep here tonight.

I grabbed a pillow and blanket from the end of the bed and tossed it onto the bench. I closed the door behind me in the bathroom and removed my clothes. My body moved slowly, but the day's events rapidly bombarded my mind. Under the warmth of the water, I took a deep breath and closed my eyes to let my thoughts become submerged. I tried to remind myself to breathe.

It is only one night.

My eyes jolted open at the sound of the door opening and Derek stumbling into the room, naked and wild-eyed.

Confused, I muttered, "What are you doing? You can't be in here."

I wrapped my arms around my body to hide my form. Without a word, Derek opened the shower curtain and stepped inside.

My words unmoved him, so I said louder, "Derek, what are you doing? You can't be here. Go back to bed!"

He sat down in the shower and began to cry. I tried to get him back on his feet, but he was deadweight.

"Derek, you drank too much. You can not be in the shower with me. Go back to bed," I said as if talking to a small child.

His cries abruptly stopped. I was relieved, reaching down again to help him step out of the shower. Derek grabbed my arms and pulled hard, leveraging himself to stand. Without a word, he shoved my body down against the side of the tub, knees slamming into the wet floor. Derek twisted my arms behind my back, pushing my face into the shower curtain. The weight of his body pressed hard into mine, my chest bruising against the side of the tub. Water dripped into my eyes.

I began to scream, unable to pull my arms out of his grasp, "Stop! Please stop! Please stop! Oh, God, no."

He did not relent. Instead, he continued to force himself closer. I was not strong enough to pull myself away. In his drunken stupor, Derek began to show frustration by pulling his body further from mine but kept a tight grip around my wrists. His hands on my arms loosened, and they fell heavily to my sides with a resounding thump. The shower water still rained down around me. Derek's body straightened, and he stumbled out of the bathroom.

The weight of my body felt endless as I carried myself out of the shower, crawled to the door to secure the lock, and collapsed to the floor. Gasping for air and trembling, I wrapped a towel around myself. I lowered the toilet seat, making a pillow with my arm and resting my head on top. The cold tile surrounded my crumpled legs, folded in like a wounded mermaid. My stomach turned sharp within me. I wanted to vomit, but I was empty. I was a stranger in my skin, transparent and numb. The beating of my heart pounded loudly against the sides of my head. I closed my eyes to keep out the pain and shake the memory into darkness. The dampness of my hair mingled with tears, and I put a hand on my cheek to wipe it away.

I could not feel its warmth or form. There was no feeling left. My body gave beneath me, exhausted from the struggle and fear. I wanted to close into myself and be reborn, made clean. I begged for rest from the God whom I had denied help. Sleep did not greet me. I was alone.

It was nearly morning when my senses returned. I needed to find a way to cover my skin and conceal my shame. I would not allow Derek the opportunity to imagine any part of my body after I was gone. As I cracked the door, the first sliver of daylight lined the tile, guiding my path to freedom. Derek was still asleep, face down, naked on the bed. Quietly fumbling through the bag for clothes, I slipped on the first thing I found before walking outside.

I will call my Mom to come pick me up. Shame enveloped me with the thought. I had no words to explain my situation. There is no worthiness to the admittance of being wronged. *Who will help me?* I stood outside the lobby door, bag in hand, waiting for an answer that never came. Without hope, I sat down on the curb outside the hotel. I crawled inside myself, silent. Apathetic.

The sun was high in the sky when Derek pulled the car around to where I was sitting. I did not see him leave the hotel room or walk to the pool hall to retrieve the car. Without a look or a word, I put my bag in the backseat and opened the passenger door to step inside.

"I have been driving all around here looking for you. Where have you been?" he asked, sounding annoyed.

I said nothing. My head was as heavy as my heart. Without a word, I continued looking straight ahead. My body ached. I was lost in my mind as the music blared. Hours had disintegrated by the time Derek pulled the car into the driveway. I immediately opened the door, desperate to be untethered from his presence. Before I could slam the door, I turned around to ask, "Are you not going to say anything about what you did to me last night?"

"What are you talking about? Nothing happened last night," came the answer. He stared at me, challenging me to say differently.

My chest seized. I reached into the back of the car to grab my bag and slammed the door shut. *That was the last time I would let myself be hurt. That was the last time I would see him. I already forgot about him.*

Chapter 6

I chose an open chair on the fourth row from the back of the church. Thinning cushions outlined indentations where many had sat before me, hands folded in fervent prayer. I ran my fingers along the smooth, curved edges of the metal frame and wondered if today would somehow be different. Above, insignificant windows mocked me, serving as a snapshot of freedom beyond the barren blocks of white cement. The naked walls lost purpose as they stood ashamed next to the striking opposition of brick-colored carpet. It was a quaint enough room, no larger than the apartment I recently began renting downtown. After the incident with Derek, I sold my car and moved closer to the city. I would not be wounded again if I could not be found.

Mapping out the dimensions of the space, I figured the quickest way to escape unnoticed was to take two subtle right turns and pace thirteen steps straight back until I reached the double doors. Unfortunately, just as I had finished my calculations, the music sounded from the meager stage. When I looked around, I noticed the seats remained only spotted with faces. I was outside of the camouflage of familiarity, not even remotely hidden. I was trapped. Someone would discover me any minute. I stood with the few people who sang along to the lyrics. I closed my eyes and felt my chest rise until I could no longer hold the air in my lungs, and I slowed my exhale. Tiny pulsations of anxiety pricked the hair on my arms to stand on end. I had made a mistake coming here.

A once-Christian, I was a lukewarm picture of pure, American-bred triumph. Years prior, I felt certain of a place called home. It was the church. But, my identity was shaken, and I was left with a strand of unknowns. So, I found myself crawling back to the basking warmth of the eternal sunshine of religion. It was an awkward loneliness, starting over among people you had just met, yet, in the same sentence, would call you "sister."

    Growing up in the cultural Christian south came with an upper hand over the folks who had never had the privilege of filling out a welcome card. You learned the customs and language and the ritualistic potlucks. I attended church activities six days a week in middle and high school. Legalism was a chore, a checklist, and a remarkable prison that lent itself to building a wall around the one who fashioned it. In due fashion, proper responses and unspoken rules were administered. The church beamed pridefully, hosing down dirty members before receiving them into the bathtub. I am sure church kept me out of a lot of trouble, but it left me with more questions than people had answers. Saying "I don't know" was not viable in the small town where I once belonged. Instead, people kindly made you feel guilty for your lack of faith if you questioned anything outside the cultural normality. Ignorance took its throne and named itself King of the South.

    As a child, I earnestly immersed myself in Scripture, finding solace in the pages. I prayed fervently and sang with all that was within me. I signed the card, even the one where I promised not to drink, smoke, listen to music with unsavory lyrics, or have sex before marriage. If I followed the rules, Jesus would love me. I would belong to a family of Christians caring for me, and I would find a husband who would honor and respect me. And yet, privilege has a way of distorting religion, twisting it to make it her own. I should effortlessly see that written throughout the pages of the New Testament. Somehow, shockingly, I missed it, just like the Pharisees.

    Jesus walked among His neighbors, saying this scripture is fulfilled in your hearing today.[5] I have come to bring you completion. I am Your Messiah. You don't have to wait any longer. You know me.[6] People who had touched his face, spoken to his mom, watched the ticks of wood notch off as he grew taller each year missed it. Completely. Somehow, in the familiarity of it all, we all miss it. We miss Him.

    I was still lost in thought when I noticed the pastor

standing uncomfortably close. The church service had been over long enough for a few people to meander out the door. I was still sitting in the same position as when it began, arms folded tightly across my chest.

"Hey, Christine, we're so glad you were able to make it," Pastor Bill said.

"Thank you. Me, too," I lied. I shook myself from my thoughts and smiled upward toward him.

Pastor Bill is a regular at the coffee shop where I work, and I felt it was time to pay him the same courtesy of solicitation. He wore thick black glasses that emboldened his stark white hair. His frame was modest. Unpretentiously, he always introduced himself as Pastor Bill. If he was not so pleasant, I am sure it would bother me that there was a need to express a title before the name chosen by his mother. It was more of an identity and less of a role. Bill extended the invitation to attend his church as often as I handed him a cup of coffee. Now, after examining the status of his congregation, my curiosity was aroused as to whether I needed a church or whether his church needed more warm bodies to cover the seats.

I noticed a few other familiar faces as the chairs were empty. These same people frequented the coffee shop, but not many left tips.

"You'll join us for lunch?" he asked more as a polite expectation than a question.

"What?" I was caught off guard. I forgot about the potlucks. My mind was wrapped around referring to oneself as a collective; we're so glad you could make it.

"*We* have lunch prepared each week in the fellowship hall just down the stairs," Pastor Bill continued.

I cringed. *Fellowship* hall? The word left me slightly nauseous, and I felt like running away from the conversation without speaking another word. Self-controlled, I maintained I had work to attend to, but I appreciated the invitation.

Walking out into the sunshine, the gravel churned beneath my shoes. I heavily exhaled as if I had been holding onto my breath the entire service. The people there were nice enough, I thought.

Everyone needed someplace to begin again.

That following Sunday, I found myself back in the same metal chair. I sang the songs and met a person or two. I slipped out quietly before lunch began. All things in due time.

I locked the doors of the coffee shop and hugged my co-worker goodbye. Over the last three years, the people at work opened up my world of humanity in ways I never had the opportunity to wrap my arms around. I carried all of my privilege and prejudice with me when I moved, coming from a hometown that was painstakingly composed of white, middle-class Christian families. I was delighted to learn from my co-workers, who welcomed my ignorant questions with more grace than I found in any church meeting. I listened as they told me what it felt like to grow up gay in a Christian home, to choose the practice of Buddhism and still cling to the wisdom of Jesus, to come to work dressed as a male and then leave to put on makeup and a dress because that was how they felt the most at home in their body. My co-workers invited me to parties and, without judgment, asked why I chose not to take drugs or have sex. I was welcome to talk about my experiences with the Holy Spirit and how the Bible guided me to seek Truth. We disagreed, but we stayed open to listening to each other. I learned to put down my judgment and stop trying to convince everyone to love Jesus. Instead, I asked Jesus to help me embody His love for others in the same way He spent time with sinners, prostitutes, and tax collectors while he walked around in human skin. It was a slow unfolding because love is wild and messy. These friends forced me to get my hands dirty, removing me from my comfortable prejudice to fully embrace our friendship.

Darkness had fallen, and I was exhausted from a long work day. I slumped into the driver's seat. Midway home, the phone vibrated from where I tossed it onto the passenger seat. I reached over and passively accepted the call before realizing I did not recognize the number on the screen. Expecting a solicitor or automated service, I tiredly answered, "Hello."

"You belong to me," came the voice from the other end of the phone.

"I'm sorry?" I responded, waking up from the haze.

"You belong to me now," he repeated.

I paused, catching my breath in an attempt to capture my thoughts.

"We had sex, Christine. You are mine. Haven't you read your Bible?" The voice became familiar in my mind, piecing together tone and cadence.

I gasped. *How did he get this number?*

"You're delusional, Derek. We never had sex. Do not ever call me again. I will forget you ever existed," I grasped the steering wheel as lights blurred past me. My body faded into dizziness.

"I will find you," his voice was dark and monotone.

I hung up quickly and threw the phone to the floorboard, trying to maintain my lane. Tears blurred my vision. Shallow, haunting breath waved over me, unconsciously keeping me alive. My head drowned thoughts more quickly than they could lucidly form. I loosened the steering wheel grasp, my fingers trembling as I picked up the phone and scrolled past numbers on the screen; names of people who once walked beside me through my days flickered and subsided. Family, inconvenienced by the heaviness of my story, left no room for grace to abound. I could not fake joy for them to extend acceptance. Friends, who once stood shoulder to shoulder, now refused to support the weight of my burden. I paused at Rachael's name, only long enough to admit she no longer knew what was happening in my life. *I have no one to help me.* As I continued down the road, headlights beamed into my view. *Maybe I should just run off the road and end it all now.* I imagined each car that passed veering slightly into my lane, hitting me head-on. *At least it would be over.*

I pulled the car into a vacant parking lot and threw my hands over my face, audibly gasping for air. I was alone in my fear as the darkness penetrated through the glass. In desperation, I continued searching for a light, a voice that could save me. I clicked on Pastor Bill's name and silently prayed he would respond. Far enough removed from my past, he could not be driven away by this buried shame. It was late. I was sure he was in bed asleep.

"Hello," he answered.

"Hi, Bill. Pastor Bill. I . . . I'm sorry to call so late," I cried.

"It's fine," he replied quickly. "Are you okay?"

OKAY? I didn't even know what those letters stood for. I knew I was *not* okay. The blood left my face, pumping into a heart that barely knew its functioning rhythm. The beginning was too long ago to start, and as I swam in my thoughts, the dam was released.

"Derek called," I slowed my breathing, trying to regain any sort of coherency in my speech. I could feel the slam of the tub as the dizzying whirl of memories hit hard in my chest. I didn't know where to begin.

"I thought I had blocked his number, and I didn't realize it was him when I picked up the phone. I don't know how he found me. I don't know how he got my number. I changed my phone, my car, and my home." But he *did find* me, threatening my life with lying accusations. The tears pooled.

"Slow down," Pastor Bill responded. "Can you make it to a safe place tonight?"

"Yes," I breathed out slowly. "I can go stay with my sister."

"Okay, Christine. I want you to tell me what happened," he continued. I heard the furniture creaking as he moved from his bed into another room. "I'm here to listen. You can trust me."

The overflow of my heart poured from my lips. Months of caged-in and dressed-up anger and guilt trickled out of my mouth into the earpiece. There were no eyes to peer back in judgment, so I spilled over, uninhibited by the fear that so easily entangled me. I proceeded to elaborate on the deep-seated wounds that had kept close souls in my life at arm's length. I divulged minute details at the cost of re-traumatizing my body as each memory was detailed aloud.

The lie of the enemy slashed a gaping word across my bleeding heart: *unlovable*.

Somehow, this word, this hiss, this subtle nodding of yes, permeated into the deepest refuge and created a chasm between God and myself. People, image bearers of the loving face of Love itself, now seemed distant and unsafe. The mirror twisted my own form; my eyes darkened, exposing only scars and imperfections. The choice to love unconditionally translated into a lack of boundaries. I made myself into a savior, blindly attempting to bring light into darkness when, all the while, my own soul was dimming. I praised Jesus with my lips, but the lie grew stronger in my heart.

Unlovable.

God is Love. The scripture is plain. God is love. If I am unlovable, how can I know this Love? How can the words of Jesus marry the wounds of my heart? How could the confession of myself, as a believer, be true if I could not receive God?

Unlovable.

And how could I trust those who claim they receive and revel in the glory of Christ when, out of their mouths, come verses overshadowed by curses? In the same breath, I had been duly showered. Rage laid waste to my body, but the emotional and spiritual wounds lasted long after the bruises subsided.

Unlovable.

For too many longing hours, I remained amid unspeakable abuse that lingered in the moments of quiet or stillness when the memories rushed in, unwelcome. It took me months to leave no trace for Derek and secure my personal information. In the days that followed our separation, I became paranoid, hardened, and lonely. Even far away, I lived in a constant state of fear, no longer able to walk down the street or through a store alone without my body tensing. I was a leper in my own skin, untouchable and unknown to those around me. The message echoed, hollowing the empty ravines and repeating itself against the walls into the pulses of my DNA.

Unlovable.

It felt good when I finished my confession; finally, I felt safe in a person's knowledge of me.

"Can I pray with you?" Pastor Bill asked.

I had not prayed in years, not earnestly anyway. In my shame, I sewed myself the fig leaves and walked out of the garden of His love. Church taught me to come clean to God in order for Him to love me and embrace me. I felt dirty, used, and alone. I was no longer suitable.

"Yeah," I muttered into the phone.

They were healing words, filled with compassion and peace. For a brief moment, I paused, allowing them to rest upon the wounds of memory. We hung up the phone, and the car engine turned over. As I drove towards the apartment, a floodgate of memories burst forth and washed away all peace. My hands were too weak, and I could not grasp the truth. I cried myself to sleep, but I was a ghost outside of my body, unable to feel the tears.

Pastor Bill called and asked to meet me at church the following day. When I entered the cozy office, he sat on a tattered couch with the Bible open. He spoke a thousand-year-old Truth and told me I was safe there.

"You don't have to hide anymore, Christine," he assured me. "This community is here for you to find healing. There are good women here." His hands glided over the pages of Scripture as he read, detailing the love of God and how He comes close to the broken-hearted. He repairs and restores. God makes all things new. I sat quietly, the voice of shame reminding me it had been my choice to go on vacation with Derek. I said no. I could have locked the bathroom door. I knew there was only one bed. I could've found another way home. I wished I had been wiser, purer, more alert. I could've stopped this from happening. *It was my fault.*

My thoughts were interrupted. "Christine, from what you've told me, I think it would be wise to get a restraining order. I can help you with the legal process."

He did not understand that this was all my fault. I knew better. If I had made better choices, I would not have been assaulted. I knew about Derek's anger. I knew about his violent outbursts. I still said yes.

"I don't think that's necessary, but thank you," I replied flatly.

Pastor Bill sighs low, "Okay, but if you change your mind, let me know. Look, I know you feel like you don't belong here, but I want you to stay. These are good people. They can help you. Will you stay?"

"Yes," I complied. "Yes, I will stay."

I did not recognize that I was crying. With fatherly tenderness, he hugged me and wiped away my tears, affirming a deeper identity within me. I was invited to start a new life in this space, with this family. Born again and again. It was painful turning in the dirt to shed this skin for new growth.

She sat on the front row, cross-legged in her chair. A

journal was propped up on her knee, and she seemed absorbed in her own world. Apart from the dark-headed boy on stage who played guitar, she appeared to be the only other person in the church around my age. Without warning, she slammed closed the book pages, bounced up from her seat, and walked across the room to the empty chair beside me.

"Hi," she smiled and stuck out her hand. "I'm Elisabeth."

"Hi, I'm Christine."

"He's cute, isn't he?" She glanced up at the stage where the guitarist was tuning his strings.

"I don't know. He's not really my type, I guess." I scrunched my nose to show her my disinterest.

Elisabeth laughed, hiding her mouth with her hand. It seemed as if there were years between us. Her childlike nature made me uncomfortable yet drew me into her innocence.

"Ryan and the pastor's daughter are dating. She's nice. I'm sure you'll meet her," Elisabeth continued unrestrained. "The women are getting together today after the service. Do you want to come with me?"

"I, uh . . . I, yeah, yes, I would," I surrendered.

Elisabeth remained beside me during the service, scribbling notes and drawing pictures as the pastor spoke. When the music began to play, she sang loudly, uninhibited, catching harmonies and waving her arms. Her voice motivated me to join in. My body eased into the worship motion, swaying along with the melody. I felt a rush of tears welling salty within the walls of my eyelids. It felt like coming home. We sat down together, and there was peace. I looked at her and smiled. She smiled back warmly.

After lunch, the women returned to the sanctuary, where a circle of chairs was formed in the center. I sat down next to Elisabeth. The lady across the circle was boisterously chatting about her marriage, vacillating between laughter and tears. Her hands waved with the pitch of her voice. Like watching a theatrical production, I unintentionally swayed along with her. Another woman in the group, meek and well-postured, fumbled through a neatly organized bag to find a pair of gold-rimmed reading glasses. She pulled her tattered and marked Bible out and read aloud a verse

I had not heard in years but was deeply familiar. I commented on the value and importance of women in marriage, their position, and their priority. The words flowed out of my mouth as naturally as if I had experienced this sort of relationship. The women nodded in agreement, and I listened to them pray. In the spaces of silence during prayer, a deep longing emerged to join this mystery of intimacy. I wanted a marriage that transcended fairytales. I wanted to be known and loved for the darkest places of my soul so they could be transformed into light. I wanted to know the kind of love Christ died for in those pages of holy text and this wayward bride He pursued. I wanted to believe we could be the people who are compelled to drink from the well and not grow thirsty.

I joined the rhythm of these meetings. Still haunted by not-so-distant memories, I stepped forward in the dance. The congregation took my hand and led my steps, graciously surrounding and teaching me slowly. Brokenness can sever the ties of trust needed to waltz confidently. So, I fumbled into position. Practice was a necessity. I fell into these people with their graciousness and vulnerability. They embraced what was left of this abused, bewildered, and fragile frame. I accepted the care, mimicking their dance. Moving, always moving, because, in the stillness, the lies grew louder.

Each week, my knees hit the sanctuary carpet as I wept aloud. God met me there, whispering healing over the feeble offering of surrender. My pain was not unnoticed by Him, and He folded me into His side. Once strong and bold, I had collapsed into myself, asphyxiated. My suffering became wrapped up in His own, a reminder God is not a distant father but One Who Knows. One Who Sees Me. My wounds bled out as I continued to keep them nicely bandaged for the sake of those around me. I craved to keep clean, to hold an identity that was not tied to the pages of my past relationships, mistakes, and abuse. I wanted to recreate myself, put myself back into the hands of the Potter, and plead for God to create something different.

I kept waltzing forward. The pain lessened as I became more involved, delving into studies, assessments, books, and retreats. Mostly, I felt alone as I attempted conversations with those much older than myself and learned what faith embodied, what it looks like on this side of eternity. The people appeared so clean, harboring old ties and extreme boundaries. My soul felt wasted, too vast and limitless in seeing God's nature in the world's wild things. I craved the God of my innocence, the whisper of comfort as a child, the earth stuck between my toes, the stars' reminder of my smallness, and the wild goose leading me toward flight. Within this group of shiny people, conservative politics and female modesty permeated the chatter. I had promised to stay, to keep safe here, so I choose not to withhold myself from the joy of simplicity. Like learning new ways of living from my co-workers, I began to enjoy a few of the very peculiar church people around me.

In my attempts to discuss Chesterton, Lewis, and Bonhoeffer, perplexed brows met me. But, oh, how they prayed. The church lifted its voice in prayer, vibrato notes of baritone and soprano reaching upward. I felt alive beside them when they worshiped, ringing from the sound. Singing became a healing art for me, an unhindered exploration of the words of others. What was lacking in numbers was made up for by a depth of voice. The church, she sang. It was rich and sweet, washing over me like a great flood. I stepped into the water and drank deeply.

I sat at the square table, staring into my cup. The oil formed iridescent waves atop a layer of dark liquid. I brought the ceramic mug to my lips and inhaled deeply. *This is the only way to breathe,* I think. Coffee may be an addiction to most, but my passion has always been the people coffee brings together. New and familiar faces pulsed through the doors of the coffee shop and awakened me to the soul of every given body, each one with a story to tell. My vocation held delicate tension between pouring lattes and counseling wounds. Unsure whether the true motivation lay in compassion or fascination, I listened intently, sorting through the facades to find truth in the pain of others. I was utterly intrigued, convinced to the core that coffee brought to life conversation that would otherwise never be shared. It was our morning truth serum with secrets stored inside each of us—far better than whiskey that exaggerated the world.

When Ryan looked at me from across the table and asked about my dreams, I could not find any words. I paused, remembering the countless times Ryan had entered the coffee shop. Most of the time, he sat alone, typing away behind the computer screen's glow. On occasion, he cautiously attempted to order what was known as the "Christine Special." My heartfelt attempts to share my caffeine addiction usually ended with people becoming comatose from sugar and dairy, with only a remnant of recognizable coffee flavor. It was no different with Ryan.

Diverting his question, I inquired about his role at the church. It was hard not to take notice of him since he was typically on stage leading the band. In the newness of stepping into a small crowd, I assumed getting to know a few people was part of the welcome basket. Ryan shared how he explored different areas of ministry, from leading the band to various community events. There was a naiveté in his conversation that was endearing, as if he'd lived an entire life sheltered from the storms of the real world. I was still trying to feel comfortable within the realm of safety, this inclusive church life.

Ryan's blue eyes pierced heavily into mine, unwavering. I hesitated before beginning, so he asked again, "What are *your* dreams?"

Slowly, the origin rose to the surface of the conversation.

The coffee shop. For years now, I had tucked it in bed. I began slowly, deliberately choosing my words as I opened up and shared:

I was barely sixteen when I heard God call my name. Over the next few years, my infatuation flared into dreams of mismatched mugs on walls, overstuffed chairs, under-read books, nights filled with dialogue on social justice, and days shot through with espresso. I tortured notebooks with drawings and potential store names, building on the steady passion that lit up my world. The dream coffee shop became my obsession. However, college has an incredible way of smoldering the wick of desire. Classes and lectures on fifty-page business plans, including financial analysis and profit projections, nearly drained me. Working forty hours a week as a barista was not sustaining my enthusiasm. While researching one afternoon, I came across a company hosting coffee tours in Central

America. With a compulsion that, up until this point, was utterly foreign to me, I signed up, emptied the little money saved in my bank account, and called my Mom to tell her I was leaving for Guatemala in a week . . . by myself.

Seared into my memory, as the plane landed, was the sight of shanty huts exposed, saved by a piece of cloth covering the windows, huddled close, and built on top of one another. A small, dark man stood at the baggage collection holding a sign with only my name, Christine. We exchanged a quick smile and greeting. Hugo. The two of us loaded up into his 4-runner and began a journey that would unknowingly change my life over the next ten days. On a narrow two-way path up the mountain, we cleared buses carrying people hanging out of the windows. "Chicken buses," Hugo called them. Crosses dotted the way, reminders of the times riders had been under the jurisdiction of less fortunate drivers. It was terrifying. I held my breath for two hours as the vehicle overtook the terrain. With one eye squinted open, I watched children play in the dirt with machetes, and emaciated cows lifted their heads slowly as we threw dirt from the tires.

The land flattened. My knuckles loosened, white from clutching the bag on my lap. A man holding a machine gun waved us closer. A tension formed around my eyes and jawline. He and my driver exchanged dialogue in a foreign tongue, and we were ushered into an open area. A few small white houses formed a circle within the farming community. Stray dogs and dirty children wandered aimlessly. We stopped abruptly, and I tore myself from the seat, sore and exhausted from the day's travel. Hugo jumped out of the car and walked to one of the houses with me. He opened the door to showcase where I would be staying. He told me he would return to pick me up in the morning, turned around, and was gone. With daylight streaming through the windows, I collapsed onto the tiny bed frame and fell into a deep sleep.

The next morning, I was up with the roosters, dressed for the unknown, and waited silently. When a knock came on my door, I quickly slipped on my shoes and stepped out into the heat.

"We will hike," Hugo explained briefly. "You will help farmers plant coffee."

Thankfully, hiking was not something to which I was unaccustomed. We walked on into eternity, the path narrowed before us. Lush foliage draped around us, and Hugo often stopped to talk about the benefits of the botanical surroundings. He folded a large leaf delicately and sipped the dew; others were described as useful for soups and medicinal benefits. A small hut had been *constructed in a clearing to overlook the other mountains. I watched as the fog rose and covered the tall trees. Below, a thin waterfall poured itself onto the ground, giving its contents to the earth.*

I thought of Eden, the perfection of good earth deteriorating quickly into toxic landfills and pesticide-infested foods. These farmers, earth workers, chose to redeem what was lost so long ago. Birth defects were reported from neighboring villages associated directly with the methods used for growing crops. The runoff of chemicals dripped from the plants into the water sources. As I listened, I noted the cycle of life. We are made of what we consume. I wanted to go back to the purity of Genesis, to drink from the waterfalls. The promise of restoration was evident within the silent goodness of the lush green and broken language between these people and myself. I felt small, and in the same breath, I was grateful for the connection between all life.

On an incline, we stopped to survey the plants growing from the fertile soil. Small green cherries poked up from the leaves, teasing. I had seen pictures of these round pods birthing beans, unrecognizable from those dumped into our machines. The process of fruit to cup carried a romance, a relationship, which heightened my awareness and deepened my appreciation of God's good earth. The man who led us unloaded his pack, emptying squares of dirt and stems. He bent low, steadied on the sloped plain, and began to dig with his hands. I looked up at Hugo, pleading for instruction. He nodded, and I understood.

With fervor, I threw down my pack and began to fill my hands with dirt. The soil was dark against my remarkably pale skin. I shoved the squared coffee child into place and covered it densely. Looking over, I noticed rows of orphaned plants waiting to be home. Sweat dripped from my brow, neck, and shoulders as they throbbed from the work. The nostalgia wore off as quickly as it had begun. While coffee plants were buried, Hugo explained how the farmers were once guerrillas, outlaws, fighting against a corrupt government. He told their story of reformation and redemption among the coffee community and how they had chosen the less profitable route by committing to organic farming. Organic and sustainable development motivated the fighters-turned-farmers to remain educated and choose what was excellent above what could make the highest income. The children's school year was based around the growing season for coffee, so there would be sufficient help in the fields. It was grueling work, the heat exhausting. The leader of our group often stopped to smile at me. With no decipherable words to deliver, I smiled back, not wanting him to feel the weight of my internal complaint. Smiling was our universal language. At that moment, I silently vowed to never take another cup of coffee for granted.

Changing the world became as simple as exchanging a morning cup of coffee for a sustainable, organic, fair-trade product. A change came down to literal change, merely cents difference. Yes, cents and sense. My vision narrowed, and passion reignited within me. I would figure out a way to take my mission into the battlefield of a small-town Georgian mentality and cut through to the hearts of the people what had been planted on my own. The farmers' voices needed to be heard and translated into a language that was easily understood by many. I would be that voice by starting my own coffee shop one day.

My chest bent into the table as I strained forward, following my words. I adjusted. Sitting upright again, I laughed nervously, apologizing for talking too much. Ryan smiled. He nodded in approval, and I relaxed into this new friendship.

"Wow, that's really cool," Ryan said, looking up from his coffee milkshake.

"I should get back to work," I admitted. "I guess I'll see you on Sunday?"

"Yeah," Ryan returned. "That'll be good. Hey, thanks for sharing your story. I can't wait to visit your coffee shop one day. It's going to be awesome."

When Ryan packed up to leave, he made his way to the cash register, where I stood, leaning against the back wall.

"You know, Christine. We could really use something like that at church," he said.

"Like what?" I walked toward him, the counter between us.

"Your coffee shop," Ryan shifted his messenger bag across his chest. "It'd be great to have a place like that at the church for everyone to meet. I bet you could make it happen."

"Huh." I stopped, my heart beating quickly as excitement built. "I've never thought about that, but I will. Thanks."

"Sure thing," he smiled. "Thanks again for the Christine Special."

I tapped gently on the door, waiting to hear if anyone was in the office.

"Come in," I recognized Pastor Bill's voice.

"Sorry to bother you. Are you busy? I can come back." My body subtly turned to the door to leave before hearing his response.

"No, it's fine. I was just working on some notes for next week's sermon." Pastor Bill removed his glasses and turned his gaze toward me.

"How are you doing, Christine?" He asked. "I've noticed you've been growing closer to Elisabeth and a few other ladies here."

"I'm really good, actually. You were right. Being here over the last couple of months has been such a blessing. I feel like I'm really growing," I responded, feeling the anxiety begin to rise in my throat. "I have a question for you," I continued hesitantly. "You see, when I graduated college, I had this vision for a coffee shop, mismatched cups, and choirs of conversation. I have been saving my money for a couple of years. It's not much, but it's enough to start something small. I've spent years believing God has given me this dream. Do you remember me telling you about staying in Guatemala?" I asked.

"Yes," Pastor Bill smiled. "Remind me what you did there."

"I spent most of my time learning from the locals, planting coffee, and seeing the process. Being with those families ignited my passion for helping undervalued workers in other countries. We have so much here in America; I just keep thinking about how much we could give away. I want to start here, at the church." I paused to breathe, my words running faster than my mind.

"How do you see that happening?" Pastor Bill asked.

"I want to start a coffee shop in the unused basement of this building, to do a complete renovation. I think it would give you all a place to meet and invite more people from the community to come to the church. There's a separate entrance. The coffee shop would be its own thing, but the church would also have permission to use it. What do you think?" I waited for an answer, holding my breath.

I saw the vision slowly igniting. Pastor Bill's eyes charged with excitement as a grin wrinkled his aging face. It was warm and contagious. Hope trickled into my skin, and I laughed aloud. He nodded slowly.

"So, that is a yes?" My lips tightened into a smile I could

barely contain.

"Yes," he said. "I think it's a great idea!"

We both stood from our chairs as he circled around the desk to envelop me with an embrace.

Pastor Bill and I spent the next week planning and working out details. When our agreement was final, Pastor Bill announced the coffee shop renovation from the pulpit. Elisabeth grabbed my hand and squeezed it softly.

"This is going to be amazing, Christine! I'm going to be here for you every step of the way," she whispered.

"Thank you, friend," I responded, squeezing her hand back.

Ryan's dad approached me after the church service. He was a large man, wearing a neatly ironed flannel shirt and work boots.

"I want to do the renovation work for you," he said in a low, kind voice.

My eyes widened.

"I do construction work on the side, and I want to offer my help. If we work together, we can have this up and going in three weeks. Of course, I can't work most days, but I can work some nights and Saturdays until it's finished. Let's sit down and talk through plans next Sunday. What do you think?"

When he finished, my face hurt from smiling. I was caught in the tension of laughter and tears where no words seemed sufficient to express emotion, so I stepped toward him and wrapped my arms around his large waist.

"Thank you," I could barely make out the words with my face buried in the soft fabric.

Ryan's dad laughed gently and said, "I believe in you. You've got an amazing gift." He wrapped his arms around me and looked down into my eyes. I saw similarities to my dad and allowed my heart to believe he would be proud, too.

My heart was still aching, but I kept reaching out my hands to God, saying, *I want to be used for Your hidden Kingdom*. His Kingdom, the invisible whispering through everything seen. I stretched out my hands; I could not help but think there was something to this interwoven community of strange family members. My fear was overwhelmed by the anticipation of stepping out. If not for a conversation over coffee, I would have kept my thoughts inside forever. It took years for me to listen to The Spirit's continual prompting to *move forward*. Ever so quietly, I began to pay attention to the desires, the patterns, and the words that poured out. In those still moments where I was not allowed to sail my own ship, the heavy winds took captive my hands, and I forced them upward and outward in praise.

Here's the white flag—submission as the act of surrender.

I laid on my yoga mat in Child's Pose, hands extended, my forehead pressed against the rubber. Defeat and surrender took on the same posture but held a different attitude. There was a shift in my spirit as I lay there, feeling my breath open my ribs and soften my heart. The rhythm of my breath became my prayer. Surrender is a practice, an active rebellion against defeat. A choice not for naive optimism but for fierce hope to arise. I flipped my palms up and received.

Chapter 7

It was late when I arrived. The desolate church was placed against a backdrop of tall pines like Buckingham Palace guards, with narrow hats and sturdy legs. I pulled my car into an unmarked parking space and fumbled the keys from beneath the steering wheel. Armed with cans of leftover sage-colored paint from my apartment, the excitement of this tangible dream-become-reality began to set in slowly. Gratitude swelled as I considered that within the short interval of time in this community, I had been given the opportunity to start building out the coffee shop. Without hesitation, strangers who had barely skimmed the surface of this long-standing journey had given me encouragement, their time, and their money to help fund the project. They moved me forward amid the pain that lingered underneath my skin.

Streams of light trailed across my feet, and the anticipation quickly gave way to a jerking fear. I turned around to see a familiar boxy frame of a car whip around in the dryness and peel up a cloud of dust around me. Although still slightly confused, my body released its tension as a recognizable face emerged.

"Ryan?" The word jumped out.

"Hey," he smiled broadly, catching his name as if it hit him for the first time. "I . . . uh . . . I thought you could use some help. Dad told me you'd be here tonight." Ryan noticed the perplexed look on my face. "I'm sorry, did I scare you?"

I realized my face was locked in confusion, and I released the creases of my forehead. "Oh, yeah, I guess you did. A little. I wasn't expecting anyone else to be here, is all."

We laughed and then walked together in silence toward what would become the entrance of my coffee shop. The downstairs of the old church had already been gutted, preparing for the new beginning. Stripped walls and wood slats stood waiting to be made into something beautiful. They welcomed us as we stepped inside. I looked around at the mess and potential and could not help but smile as joy emerged from inside.

"Well," I said as if waking from a dream state. "Here she is; let's get started!" I commanded graciously.

I handed Ryan a paint can, and he searched for something to pry off the lid. I strategically peeled the blue tape into long strips and formed them in straight lines throughout the hallways. I made no room for further conversation with Ryan, turning on the speakers to play music loudly. In the presence of men, I had learned to close myself off, not wanting to be seen or noticed, not wanting to be harmed. I tucked my head down and focused on the task at hand. Alone in my thoughts, I began to feel extraordinary tension arise in my shoulders and lightning down through my hands. The same pain that continued to haunt me since the night with Derek.

I was standing in a stall in the girls' bathroom, taping off the door, when I yelled through the wall, "Why are you here?"

"Because this is your dream," he responded. "It's awesome. I've been doing work like this with my dad for as long as I can remember. He's taught me a lot about construction. I figured you could use some help. Besides, I wouldn't be here if I didn't believe in your vision. We need something like this to change things up around here."

"Yeah," I agreed. "I want this to be somewhere that people can come together, you know . . . to talk about things that matter. That's what coffee does, I think. It just has a way of bringing people together."

Stepping out of the bathroom, we stood facing the other, paintbrushes in hand, eyes locked. I shifted my gaze downward, fearing I'd stepped over a boundary of my own vulnerable heart. I shared too much. Ryan, seemingly unaffected, diligently began working on the rest of the walls. Like a breeze through a cracked window, Ryan began to ask a few questions about my plans for the space. We both relaxed into conversation as he kept a safe distance.

Piecing together history, I learned Ryan's family had been a part of the community for years. The congregation was tightly knit, and each person held a responsibility that extended into the others' lives. Ryan wore many hats: teaching, leading music, and configuring graphic design. As he talked about his life, I acknowledged how vastly different our journeys had been up until that point, and I coveted the shelter of his days. It reminded me of a more innocent time, shaded and protected from the darkness of the insidious lie of *unlovable* beneath my veins. Being around Ryan made me feel like it was possible to become childlike again. As our conversation waxed, I found myself laughing and opening up to a friendship I never expected.

Ryan and I traded our newest music interests and the older bands we enjoyed. By the end of the night, the songs sank into melancholy. Without distraction, denying the chaos of emotion felt in each lyric was increasingly difficult.

I was immersed in the song when Ryan announced, "I guess you heard I broke up with Pastor Bill's daughter."

"Oh my gosh, Ryan. I'm so sorry. No, I hadn't heard. When did that happen?" I asked, thinking about how happy Elisabeth would be.

"Just a few days ago. It's been a long time, but I finally had the courage to let her know. She's young," he continued, "and pretty immature. We both agreed we needed to figure out what we wanted to do with our lives. It was a mutual decision."

"Well, that sounds really healthy," I laughed, thinking about the many ways my relationships had ended so poorly.

Ryan smiled and cocked his head to the side, narrowing his eyes.

"I've just never really had a healthy break-up, I guess you could say," I faked a grimace.

Ryan laughed, "I'm happier now that it's over. These last few days have been really good."

He stared at me, and I was exposed. I wanted to tell him he didn't know my story, the weight of shame I carried. I told myself we could be friends with this newfound knowledge, even with how he looked at me.

With each stroke of paint splattered on the bathroom

wall, more details of our lives unfurled. The color smoothed itself and became alive with our exchange. This thick wall, garnished with heavy stone, had been under construction for many years. Vines grew thick as they tangled around the lie that held me here. *Unlovable.* My wasted relationship history left me guarded and insecure, choosing mostly to expose the cracks with one hyper-attention-seeking tactic after another. Words spilled out, brash and staccato, revealing the condition of my battered heart as I tried to piece together how to choose vulnerability and authenticity in the face of desiring intimacy. I was afraid.

I recalled a pastor telling me this story:

At one point in history, the glassmakers of Italy found a problem because of unscrupulous dealers. The process of making delicate dishes consisted of subjecting the substance to severe heat. Often, a piece of china came out of the oven with cracks and could not be sold as perfectly. However, many dealers used an invisible wax to coat the cracked surfaces.

The buyer could not distinguish between the good and the bad product at a casual glance. The crack could be seen only by holding the plate up to the sun. So, the honest dealers banded themselves together and devised the use of a stamp to be applied on all good pieces. This stamp bore the mark – "sine cera," or "without wax," from which we get our English word "sincere."

I stood, hands spotted with paint, exposing myself to the sun, hoping to receive a stamp of approval. I was moving toward the dream I had been pursuing for five years. A broken vessel, sealing myself with wax in order to prove myself sincere to those around me. I rubbed Scripture verses into my skin, fancy words, and interesting stories to try and soothe the imperfections created by my sin and the sin of others that left me hollow. The endless search for the balm of Gilead.

The story the pastor man told ended with this note of warning:

Often, when the patched-up dishes were exposed to the heat, the wax would melt, and the flaw was revealed. The fiery trials very often reveal the wax of our insincerity.

I was keenly aware I was stepping into the fire.

Over the course of a week, Ryan met me at the church after my shift at the coffee shop. We sat on the floor cross-legged beside one another, quiet for a minute, feeling the tension quicken. How he looked at me when I was not fully attentive began to feel desirous. My face flushed with wild unknowing. A flicker of desire forms deep in my stomach, and I lacquered over it with the reminder of my inability to trust myself. It had been less than a year since Derek had called, leaving the words hanging in the air, "I will find you." My heart lay open, gaping, bloody. The shock of Derek's words numbed the moments with Ryan. I wondered how Ryan could be around me without seeing the depth of my pain, my guarded walls, and my bleeding wounds. His eyes lingered a while longer, and the torment of attraction is pacified by shallow breath.

"I'm unprepared," I said quietly. "I never was prepared for this."

"What do you mean?" Ryan asked, wanting to hear my words. I intended to talk about the coffee shop, my dreams, and our progress. Instead, I realized I could not hide my feelings if I continued to speak, "It's nothing." I closed myself off from spilling over the contents of my heart.

I vowed not to allow myself to feel the weight of his look, the cost of his words. I knew my desire was not for this man. It was to be loved within myself—truly, intentionally loved. To the extent that we can be known by another is the true test of our ability to receive love. So, I closed myself off to the possibility.

"I just mean, I didn't think the coffee shop would come together this quickly. That's all." My eyes shifted, fearing to give themselves away.

"You're an amazing poet," he blurted out.

"How . . . how do you know that I write?" I asked, bewildered.

"I found something of yours. I mean, I have something for you. I hope you don't mind; I stole your words," Ryan continued, getting up from the floor where we both sat like stone.

Like many afternoons prior, we spent the last four hours sanding down drywall and sealing concrete. Ryan's dad had completed much of the construction, contributing countless days alongside me. I accepted this as my new home as the walls went up and the counters were strategically placed. My hair was covered in wood chips, and my hands felt like they were becoming sandpaper. But my heart softened as it swelled with gratitude.

Most of our time was spent at church, lacquering floors and patching drywall. Ryan's Dad, Derek, took on the coffee shop as though it was his second job, sacrificing long hours and an even longer drive to complete this dream. His enthusiasm was refreshing and kept me motivated to continue the pursuit. Couches were purchased, and art was hung on the walls. My sister, April, told me once as a kid that if you write down your dreams, they would become your goals. After exhausting classes and bitter nights, *Origin* would soon be open for business.

"Follow me," Ryan commanded.

Ryan led me out of the building through the exposed sheetrock and dusty floors. The air was thick but fresh. It was surprisingly dark when we stepped outside, the days seeming to string together like a wild ride. Behind the church was a smaller building, old but barely touched. It was mostly used for storage of abandoned pews and worn-out hymnals. We walked across a makeshift bridge that led to the door. Ryan unlocked it and noisily secured its place against a post. I stopped and looked at him, confused. He smiled, childlike. Distrust sprung up in me, and I felt my shoulder tense as the remembrance of pain returned. The memory of Derek flashed in my mind, the door of the bathroom opening. I took a deep breath of pine and reminded myself that Ryan was not Derek. He was safe.

I followed Ryan inside; the room was musty. The smell of mothballs stayed heavy. I pressed the door to remain wide, breathing in the hot air from outside. Ryan sat at a distressed piano packed in tightly against the far wall. Without looking at me, he pulled a fragment of paper from the back pocket of his jeans. Neatly pressing the corners, the paper adjusted against the side of the keys. The notes came out clear and confident against the empty space. With an unusual boldness, Ryan continued to work through the piece. His fingers moved alongside the keys as lovers danced in sync.

He began to sing. The silent night was pierced as familiar words fell over me. The words were mine, lines from a tucked-away poem reinvented. Beauty from ashes.

Tears spilled down my cheeks as the realization became alive within me. Those secret places that existed in lines of poetry and prose—they were the truest version of myself. While Ryan played, he sang over me my own pain and my own healing. My heart awakened again to love. I unfolded. I received. I stood at the door, and I was changed. The light, the sound, and the experience morphed into a moment of newness. He finished the piece, a silence thickened around us. Still seated, Ryan turned his eyes toward mine, asking for my response and approval. Attention. I wiped away my tears and attempted to smile. There were no words; I felt unprepared for this feeling that had no name.

"That was beautiful," I fumbled. "Thank you."

"They're your words," Ryan responded. "I just put music to them."

"You did," I muttered under my breath, barely able to make sense of myself.

We walked away from the intimacy of the moment without touching. It felt strange not to embrace. I knew myself well enough to keep my hands buried deeply against my sides so as not to give away false intentions. I walked away empty yet filled to the brim with a newness of seeing myself within my own words. For years, I managed the building of these walls, isolating parts of myself that became so foreign that I barely recognized myself when another showed to me. In that tiny space, rural and unkempt, I was found. It was an unearthing from a stranger, deep and mysterious, like the apocalypse, the revelation of self-love.

After Sunday's service, Ryan invited me to a picnic. A well-deserved break from the weeks of work together, I jumped into the passenger seat of his Jeep.

"Have you been to the beach near here?" Ryan prompted.

"No, but I'm glad we're going. I need something new." I pulled myself up into the seat and settled in.

Pulling a bottle of bubbles from my bag, I threw my legs up on the dash. Since I moved out of Alyssa's house, I had not smoked a cigarette. I extended the bubble wand slowly from the glassy film and exhaled through the ring. A strand of iridescence fell behind us as I let go of everything that hindered me from feeling alive. I was learning to breathe again, a simple inhalation and exhalation that allowed my body to exist. I had grown my hair out since I left Derek, and the strands whipped around my face as we took off down the unending road, no one in sight. In the wild heat of summer, I gave myself over to the wind and laughed loud and long.

Ryan smiled, "You're crazy."

"I know. I like it that way," I said.

"Me, too," he looked over from the driver's seat and shifted gears.

We both fell a little deeper into knowing.

Ryan pulled the Jeep onto the sizzling tarmac. I grabbed our lunches from behind the seat, anxious to dig my toes into the warm sand. Hiding my face behind thick sunglasses, I silently hoped my glinting eyes wouldn't give too much away. The last few projects had been completed, and respite was welcome. I resigned to the beating waves and pulled a soda from the cooler.

My soul, mangled from the mess of my past, wearily received the water. Living Water, which Jesus offers, only comes when you accept it. Fully. In this time of wandering, I was desperately thirsty. My body ached. I heard the Word, the Truth of His whispering. The Truth comes in songs, verses, sermons, and communion. But it was also found here at the beginning of a relationship, the steady pulse of the waves and the gentle recognition of God's image stamped on each person alive, including myself. I hid my eyes for so long from looking into the mirror I forgot that I, too, was wonderfully and fearfully made. I sat still, and for the first time, I noticed that my thoughts did not immediately flash back to fear. *Be still and know that I am God.[7] Be still and know that I am. Be still and know. Be still. Be.* I recognized it as an old nursery rhyme. It soothed; it comforted. It gave me a moment of sweet reprieve, and it was gone again in an instant. My fists clenched, determined, and the Living Water ran right through. I turned toward Ryan and craved his attention.

Ryan sat down next to me and began stringing together fragments of his history. He told me about the implications of dating the pastor's daughter. She had become an acquaintance since committing to the mixed pot of a community where I was now planting roots. She and I could not be more dissimilar. The pastor's daughter embodied the fairytale story, awaiting Prince Charming to take her away. She was feminine, naive, and deeply pocketed into her dad's side. It seemed fitting that she and Ryan had a long-standing relationship. They embraced their shelters while I prematurely extended my wings, tumbling from the safety of the nest built for me. I allowed my imagination to take hold, and I saw the two of them dancing out into the lights and sounds of wedding bells, a future white picket fence with two children and another on the way.

"I'm really sorry things didn't work out. It seems you've both moved on. At this point, I just can't imagine having a husband or kids. I think I've learned in the last year, it's just not meant to be for me. For me, it's just the coffee shop," I sighed deeply, allowing fear to speak for me. My thoughts sounded convincing, unrehearsed. The heart is deceptive. Ryan skeptically examined my face to see if there was any leniency in my dream. When he looked at me, some part of me gave. A slight pull rendered the wall of my heart, and I heard the music that Ryan played that dark night—the night when I began to feel again. The veil through which I saw him lifted, transfiguring a familiar face and awakening desire.

"I think I can change your mind," Ryan spoke assuredly.

Time slowed enough to hear the whisper *unlovable*, and I waited for the inevitable crash. An old friend's words rose: *you love being in love*. I conceded. Love disguised and resounded loudly in the form of an unfamiliar kiss. I dove into the murky water. I washed myself away from the life I once led, the abuse, the harsh words, the sin, and the lust for attention. All was temporarily salved, thick paste masks on a wound too deep for stitching.

We kissed.

Against expectation, the euphoria lasted into wordy nights. Days rained, flooding into the next. We built our boat, gathered our suitcases, and enclosed ourselves in our emotions. So, this is what it is to finally be loved. I smiled thickly. With much left unhealed, I plunged into a new beginning, trusting this man to be responsible for what he ignited within me.

Falling in love always left me with the impression that, at some point, you would hit bottom. This feeling of love, however, clouded my mind with weightlessness.

The ease with which the door opened surprised and delighted me. The giddy excitement lingered, and we talked until all hours of the night, exchanging short breaths between words and steady laughter. The lie of being unlovable was vanquished under the adoration Ryan held with each passing glance.

Chapter 8

Amid the excitement, a neighboring church invited Elisabeth and me to join them on a trip to Colombia. I gladly accepted. We boarded a plane with unfamiliar faces, nestled into the safety of one another.

"I'm happy for you," Elisabeth smiled. She held my arm as a daughter would her mother.

"Thanks," I said. "I'm really happy. It's been a long time since I have felt anything but sadness. It feels good."

We talked and laughed for the duration of the plane ride, scheming future plans of us working together at Origin, the coffee shop. She joked about Ryan and me getting married, and I tried to minimize the sudden longing that surfaced from under my ribs.

"Ryan is a good guy," Elisabeth continued. "He would never hurt you."

"I know," I replied. "I can't tell you how much it means for you to know that, too."

Our plane landed in a bustling city, much different than my experience in Guatemala. We were surrounded by swarming Americans determined to "bring Jesus" to the people of Colombia (as though He was secretly packed away in our suitcases). I was there for the coffee. And the children. The smiles of the kids I met on the farms in Guatemala and their incredulous faces were at the forefront of my mind. I wanted to be close to people unlike me, to hear their stories and touch their hands. A team of us would help reconstruct a school that had recently received funding for the project. When we arrived at the local college where we stayed, it felt luxurious compared to the ghettos we passed. Heavy gates shut us inside to protect us from the very people we came to serve.

Our team was led to the dormitories, where we bunked and shared showers, a first-world sacrifice.

I walked outside the gates to dirty children begging on the corners; their dark eyes were filled with sadness and charm. The team dined at a crepe restaurant downtown on our second night there. After our meal, we walked toward the bus that took us back to the dormitory. The day's work was laborious, mortaring bricks and wheeling rocks. I had become accustomed to the physical labor after working on the renovation plans for Origin. I took my seat next to the window when I heard our group leader yelling from outside, "Everyone inside, get down on the ground!"

I crouched to the floor, wrapping my arms around my knees, forming a ball, and lowering my head. Head and heart covered, I shielded what was most vulnerable. Others shuffled to find their places on the bus and took shelter within their own arms. Silent breath surfaced after being held tightly. I closed my eyes and prayed for Ryan. I saw his tight jawline and piercing blue eyes shooting out from his dark hair. His kiss. I held onto the image and prayed God wouldn't take me.

When the threat of danger passed, I was surprisingly calm. I adjusted myself out of the fetal position, pressing my spine against the back of the seat. Taking in a huge breath, I exhaled loudly. *Breathe.* A boy my age was sitting next to me on the bus. His presence took me by surprise. He turned to me, and I felt as if I was staring at Alex's face. I was thirteen again and breathless. He leaned close to me, eyes wide, and touched my back. I involuntarily jumped beneath his touch.

"Are you okay?" he asked, craning his neck to look at my downcast eyes.

"Yes, thank you. Sorry, you surprised me. Do you know what just happened?" I asked, trying to shake the feeling of being small.

"Bomb threat," the boy who was not Alex responded.

"What's your name? You seem a little shaken. You sure you're alright?"

"Christine," I responded quickly. "I am fine, really. I didn't know anyone was beside me with my head down."

"I'm Joshua. We all pretty much know each other from our

church. You and your friend came from Atlanta, right?" Joshua's hand was still on my back, and my shoulders softened under the weight.

"Yes. Her name is Elisabeth," I stammered. "My friend." I looked around to make sure Elisabeth made it safely on the bus. She was seated four rows ahead of me, and her dark, asymmetrical haircut caught my eye.

"Sorry," I said. "I guess I do feel a little disoriented. A bomb threat? Does that happen often?"

"Yes, unfortunately, it does with groups like ours. What do you mean, disoriented? Are you dizzy?" Joshua asked.

"No, no, I don't think so. I'm fine. There was an illusion of safety where we'd been staying and the places we'd eaten. I guess this trip is just a lot different than the last one I went on, and I feel a little out of place." My hands shifted onto my knees as if covering them for protection. My legs felt heavy against the seat. I began to feel the slide of Alex's hands press against my skin. I wanted Joshua to stop talking to me, to get up from the chair, and to make space for Elisabeth. I wanted not to hate him because he reminded me of my past.

"I have a boyfriend," the words fell out of my mouth, and I wanted to shove them back inside.

"Really?" Joshua remains seated, casually interested. "Tell me about him," he continued without hesitation.

For the next twenty minutes, I talked about my relationship with Ryan. I included how we met, his excellent resume, and the song he played the night I began to feel again. Joshua listened and nodded with the understanding of a close friend. The bus stopped as the gates to the university clank heavily against the railings, a most welcoming entrance.

We exited the bus, and I said something to the point of nice to meet you. Elisabeth and I closed in on each other and walked to where we stayed with a few other women from the trip. She immediately launched into an interrogation about Joshua with all necessary questions needing answers: "Is he single? Do you think he is cute? What is he like?"

I laughed and told her, "I don't really know. I probably freaked him out. I guess I didn't let him talk very much."

We settled into our bunk bedroom, the buzz of anxiety was still electric in the air. As the night set in, our tired bodies slowly welcomed the thin mattresses. My mind would not give in to rest, replaying the flashback of Alex on repeat. The dormitory was quiet when I tiptoed out into the common area. I could make out tiny stars cascading across the sky between the metal bars lining the windows. *Show off.* I laughed at God, and He laughed back. When I turned the corner to the mess of chairs, I was surprised to find Joshua sitting in one of them. His back was turned, and I hesitated. Hearing the shuffling of my too-large feet, he turned and smiled.

"Have a seat," he said.

"Thank you. I'm sorry if I disturbed you. I didn't think anyone else would be awake. I couldn't sleep. It's a common problem these days," I replied.

"Want to talk about it?" Joshua asked.

"Not really," I lied. "I just feel pretty lonely here."

"Here?" he pried.

"Well," I responded. "Pretty much anywhere. The night has a way of reminding me."

"Can I tell you a story?" Joshua asked.

"Of course," I said, grateful to stop talking.

Joshua sat back comfortably in his chair, like a counselor in session, yet also the one in need of counsel. He folded his hands across his waistline and divulged intimate details of his last broken relationship. With blatant honesty, Joshua spoke of the manipulation of a younger girl, stealing her virginity. With it, her dignity. He justified it all beneath the guise of spiritual marriage after being given authority in a church setting to pastor at a young age. After a few months of living in hiddenness, Joshua was not willing to commit his life to her, only his body. She left. He whips himself daily with regret, torturing himself for his sin. Not one who is short on words, I was stunned into silence at his willing confession.

"Why are you sharing this with me?" I finally asked.

"You told me today about your relationship with Ryan and your desire for purity and honesty. Is he honest, Christine? Would he tell you if he had messed up like I did?" Joshua looked at me, intently waiting for a response.

"I . . . I don't know. I'm sure he would. We all have our past regrets," I said, trying to make sense of the conversation.

"Wouldn't you want to know if he had been with someone else? If he is with someone else?" Joshua continued.

"I trust he would have told me that. We're committed to honesty. I've been lied to before and don't think I could handle it again. He knows how important that is to me." Joshua's forward remarks made me uneasy, so I stood up from the chair, "Hey, thanks for sharing your story. I need to try and get some sleep before tomorrow's work."

I walked away, feeling the weight of Joshua's words wrap around my thoughts.

"Goodnight," he said behind me.

"Goodnight," I responded without turning back.

It was late when I called. Ryan answered the phone, groggy. "Hey, babe. Man, I've been waiting to hear from you. How are you?"

I was a mess.

"I'm fine. I just had a strange conversation with someone here, and I just needed to talk with you," I said.

"Really? Who was it?" Ryan asked.

"That's not super important right now. This may sound weird, but you and Pastor Bill's daughter never had sex, right?" I asked bluntly.

"Gosh, no!" came the answer.

I sighed.

"I didn't think so. It's just really important to me that we don't keep things from one another. I'm still healing from a lot that I'm sure we'll talk about eventually, but I just need to know you value the same things I do. I have to know you'll be honest with me, and I need you to know that I am not having sex with you unless we get married," I stated firmly.

"Of course," he said. "I've told you everything, and of course, we won't have sex until we're married."

"Okay," I said. "I trust you. We'll talk again tomorrow. I love you. I'm sorry I woke you," I whispered into the receiver.

"I love you, too." There was a click and silence. I could not shake my discontent as I lay awake in bed.

In the morning, Elisabeth and I were put on a team with Joshua. I avoided him completely. We sweated in dirty streets, stacking bricks and visiting churches. We discussed Jesus as our hope as I struggled to find my own. I met the little boy whom I had been sponsoring in order for him to continue to attend the school we were helping build. The younger kids in his class stroked my hair and skin and asked me for "provisions."

"You're white," one of our Colombian leaders said to me when I asked him what provisions were needed. "You're American. They think you have rice and food for them if you're here."

My heart broke in a million places, and I felt sick for believing my pain amounts to anything compared to their stories. Our team leader drove us around the city. He spoke plainly about what it was like to grow up as a child in Colombia. Drug rings. Poverty. Inadequate work for parents. Prostitution. Guerilla warfare. I was far from knowing the same things lurked outside my door at home. Safety is a grand illusion. These kids smiled and laughed and played and fought just the same. We hugged a million tiny necks, and I silently prayed for each of them, feeling self-pity over this life I was leading. I wanted to guard, feed, and wash their tiny hands and cheeks to give them one clean kiss. I wanted better opportunities for them. I promised myself I would learn Spanish and come back—adopt those without a home. It was a noble distraction from the gentle ache of betrayal that burned in my chest. My savior complex and privilege bled out, and my white tears helped no one.

Joshua and I talked more during our time together. He built on his story, and we discussed opening the coffee shop. There was confidence in his convictions and the ownership of his past. I found strength in his boldness and the power of accepting forgiveness. My conviction of helping these communities through coffee partnerships was stronger than before. This was my opportunity to make things right.

The night before we left Colombia, I called Ryan. I was charged with passion and began to launch into all of the experiences of the last few days. When words slowed, I noticed Ryan was not responding on the other end of the phone.

"Hey, is everything okay?" I asked.

There was a silence that spanned our distance, and I feared I knew the answer.

"There was a girl," he confessed after a long pause.

"You slept with her," I said to him.

"We had sex," his voice was quiet, "a lot."

"Why didn't you tell me when I asked you the other night?" I stretched the tension from my neck by leaning my ear to my left shoulder. Slowly, I closed my eyes and tilted to the right. Deep inhale. "I don't care what you've done, but I thought you would have at least been honest with me before you made me ask you."

Exhale.

"I didn't think it was a big deal. It was a long time ago," Ryan justified.

"That's it? That's all you have to say about it? About her?" I asked.

"Yeah, she didn't mean anything to me. It's not a big deal," he repeated.

We sat in silence. The only sound was the whistling of air through my nostrils as I exhaled deeply, trying to maintain a rhythm of breath. I sat against the wall, trying to gain composure in the hallway before entering our group sleeping arrangement. He was Adam, covered in shame and denying his leaves. I was open about my past to Ryan and poured out my wounds and shame. In our shared moments, I explained my need for transparency in order to maintain stability. I exposed all guilt and violation, bruises still faint underneath my skin. He ran away and hid, waiting for me to play God and find him.

The only exposition I could gather before hanging up the phone was, "You lied to me, Ryan. Lying is a big deal. Everyone's asleep. We'll talk about it when I'm back home."

For a brief moment, there was pleasure in his sin justifying my own wrongdoing. Justification quickly turned to disgust at the thought of him with another girl. I gathered up fragments of the innocent portrait of the person I thought I knew and tried to glue them back together in my mind. Ryan's face began to look like a third-grade art collage.

I felt like a child underneath the shallowness of my thoughts. Head on my pillow, I closed my eyes to find rest. My mind became a starving wolf. Images of this unseen girl incited seeded thought. I longed for a distraction to sleep. I stared above me. Darkness hung around my neck, and the silence was only punctuated by mouth breathing and dreaming laments.

Our givenness to another, as humans, cannot be reduced to anything less than a big deal, I thought. *To diminish sex is to take away part of our humanity invariably.* I was torn apart. *Was it not from the stage where he had lifted his voice to lead others in worship and confession?* And I lay there with the same hiss. I wondered to myself how, if he could engage a girl who *meant nothing*, how, then, would I ever know I was loved? *What will I have to give of myself?*

On the plane ride home, an older man sat beside me. He guided me gently into opening up about my hopes and fears. My words still felt unsafe in the hands of others. He shared about the death of his first wife and the choice to live open to God's love. Leon had been flying to Colombia every year to care for a community he had fallen in love with there. He did not intend to stop, and I commended him for using his retirement well. When the plane became closer to the city lights, and we began to descend, Leon asked if he could pray for me.

As we hugged and walked away, I heard his words echo loudly. *God, teach her to know you as her loving Father, to forgive her own father for where he could not love her in the ways she needed. Where she has not known love, give her love.*

Merely seven days apart, Ryan no longer held the same appeal as when we kissed goodbye. When we met at the baggage claim, he put his arms around me, his hand on the crease of my neck. I felt my back arch, attempting to rid his hands of my skin. I cried quietly, shifting my gaze away from his, distracting myself with luggage and battered small talk. Nothing prepared me for this feeling of resentment.

"What's wrong?" Ryan asked.

"It's nothing," I said. "I'm just really happy to see you."

I feigned a smile, and he drove me home.

Chapter 9

I heaved couches into their corners and arranged the tables into three small groups. A smattering of chairs held future spirits, and I could almost make out their laughter and noise. I turned the music up, alone in the church basement. Each song held a memory of Derek's apartment. My back pressed heavy against the floor, unpacking the trunk of all the memory treasures. I went back to the beginning, somehow believing I could rewrite time by re-listening to each melody in a new environment. I reinvented the song in my mind, so it was no longer tied to a memory of Derek but instead attached to the happiness I felt standing inside the coffee shop. Origin aptly named the beginning. My life was a series of starting over, always beginning again. Tonight marked the soft opening.

An espresso machine sat as a beacon of glory on top of the bar. The wood finish of the countertop had just been sealed, and a thin metal sheet stretched its length, tying in with the industrial finishes of the shop. My hands were jittery from testing espresso shots and the excitement of the night's uncertainty. I displayed homemade pastries, macaroons, and tiny cakes. At the top of the street, a crowd cheered from a local football game. Friday night's lights glared in the distance, streaming as the sun faded. I turned around, pressed my hands firmly against the tops of my thighs, and breathed in deeply as I unlocked the door and waited.

Family and friends trickled in slowly, mingling with a few folks who had stopped by from the church. People who would otherwise never cross paths exchanged words, sitting close. I kept safe behind the bar, pulling shots and frothing milk. *Keep moving forward.*

Michelle, my sister, walked up to the counter. She ordered

a latte and smiled. I handed her the drink and walked around the other side of the bar. Michelle pulled me in for a hug and whispered in my ear, "If this is the only night you are open, you have already accomplished what you set out to do." She spoke with the wisdom inherent to oldest children. "I'm glad you're here to enjoy it." She held back tears of joy.

"The work has been worth it," I responded.

"You've come a long way," she encouraged.

"Thanks," I smiled back. "I'm finally where I am supposed to be."

The rest of the evening was a blur of caffeine and conversation. Dad entered, taking up space as he sprawled on a floor chair. His six-foot-four frame extended into the middle of the space. Boisterous Puerto Rican women from the community laughed largely while a few friends from college sang along with the music on the radio. Elisabeth rounded the bar and hugged me hard, kissing me.

"You did it!" she exclaimed.

"It feels like a dream," I squealed, mimicking her pitch. "Look at these people. Never in a million years would I believe these different worlds of mine would be colliding in a coffee shop. In MY coffee shop! It's so good."

"Where's Ryan?" Elisabeth asked.

"Oh, I'm sure he'll be here soon," I replied hesitantly. He and I had not spoken much since my return from Colombia. I felt myself pulling away, choosing to wrap myself in the energy of opening the coffee shop.

The Buddhist hippie friend I lived with during college now sat beside my charismatic church leader. They began to talk about art and politics. I looked at Elisabeth, and we both laughed.

"This is my dream come true," I whispered, excitedly giggling.

Five days after the soft opening of Origin, Pastor Bill called and asked me to meet with him. I unlocked the coffee shop door and went to his office. Pastor Bill was seated behind his large wooden desk while his wife occupied an adjacent chair. He invited me to take a seat beside her. Pastor Bill's wife was a quiet, grandmotherly woman. She was welcoming but not warm. She did not join our women's meetings, so I had only ever spoken to her on occasional passes. I sat down opposite his desk like I had many times before. I was anxious to hear how they enjoyed having the coffee shop available.

"Hey, Christine. Um . . . ," Pastor Bill pursed his lips, considering his words carefully. "It has been brought to my attention that you are dating Ryan." Pastor Bill launched the discussion like a water balloon waiting to burst.

"Yes," I replied, furling my brow. "I was pretty sure you knew about that some time ago. We've been together for a couple of months. I spoke to your daughter about it before Ryan and I made anything official in our relationship. I know she dated him for a while, but she clarified that she was fine with us being together."

I stopped myself from divulging more than necessary. There was silence. I looked over at Pastor Bill's wife, whose face was devoid of expression.

"I don't know exactly how to tell you this, but he's not good, Christine," Pastor Bill finally says. "You don't need to be in a relationship with him."

"I'm sorry?" I questioned, not sure I had heard him correctly. "I don't understand. Your daughter dated Ryan for some time, and you never seemed to have a problem with it then. Look, I don't really know why we are having this conversation. If Ryan isn't good, why is he your band leader? Is there something I don't know?"

"Christine, I just need you to trust me. I invited you into this community, and this relationship is not good for you. Ryan cannot be trusted," Pastor Bill stared at me from across the desk, unwavering.

The room spun around me as I recalled the conversation with Joshua and the late-night confession. I expected Pastor Bill to divulge an egregious sin or unforgivable heresy. Instead, I was offered nothing.

My ears are ringing, "I'm sorry, but I just don't understand. Ryan has been a part of this community for a long time. His whole family has. So, if there's something he's done or something I need to know, please tell me. We've gotten pretty serious about our relationship, and I can't just leave without knowing something from you. Something specific. Are you talking about his past relationship? Because he already told me about that, and I have forgiven him. We all make mistakes."

I began to feel the same numbing sensation in my fingers like the night I stayed up with Joshua in Colombia. My shoulder ached.

"I'm sorry, Christine. I have to protect my flock. You can either end your relationship with Ryan, or you have to take your relationship elsewhere. It cannot continue at this church," Pastor Bill stated plainly.

I chewed the side of my cheek hard, trying to fight the tears.

"Well," my voice is quiet against the ringing in my ears. "It sounds like you have already made your choice."

"We have," Pastor Bill's face was unmoved.

He did not look at his wife. I understood this decision was solely his own. He and his wife had become statues, no longer human. I sat in the chair as if under their spell, not wanting to move in case the foundation would crack and break us all.

In a trance, I muttered *okay* under my breath as I walked through the office door. Only a year ago, this was a haven, a sanctuary of healing. Sitting in the same space, I had spilled my brokenness before this man. He held my story, gave me hope that my days had not been wasted, and provided an opportunity to start over. Pastor Bill had sewn a thread of redemption through the narrative of Scripture, and I believed my life could somehow be tied up in it all. The same mouth, without explanation, now insisted I was a threat to his "flock." I was once again homeless, with nowhere to belong. My ventricles ran cold with those last words, "I have to protect my flock." There was a tight pinching in my chest where my heart grappled under the weight of the Lie.

Unlovable.

I got into my car, sluggish and still spinning. A quarter mile from the church, I drove into a park entrance. I inhaled and exhaled rapidly, unable to shake the hiss, growing dizzy under the weight.

Unlovable.

Crisp autumn air sliced my lungs as I pushed open the car door. It reminded me I was still alive. *I need a cigarette.* Sitting on the swing, I called Ryan. His voicemail picked up, and I hung up the phone, sobbing heavily into my hands. After a few minutes, Ryan called, but I was already hunched over, speechless. Convulsions overtook my body.

Ryan's voice was frantic on the other end of the receiver, "Christine, take a breath. Are you okay? Where are you? What's going on?"

Finally able to compose myself, I relayed the details as they came back to mind. *He's not good . . . protect my flock.*

"He's crazy," Ryan said in a steady tone. "We've known that for a while, but he's like family. So, what can you do? We'll start over. Just me and you."

"Okay," I finally spit out. "When can I see you? I need to get out of here. I don't know where else to go. This is all I have, Ryan. I spent everything I have." I paused, feeling the weight of my world crashing against my chest. "This has been my dream for so long. What do I do with my one broken dream? What do I do with Origin?"

"Christine, we've done it once. We can build it again. You and I did all the work anyway. We don't need them." His words were convincing enough to rouse me from the swing and steer me into my car.

"I need to call my mom," I said. "I need her to come help me."

"Yeah, okay. I've got to work tomorrow, but let me know if you need anything," Ryan hung up the phone.

I stared out the windshield. The colors of the leaves turned from green to gold, losing their life. A gust of wind picked up and carried a few to the ground. This continual cycle of death and resurrection. I was still waiting to feel alive.

Mom arrived at the church the next morning, driving Dad's red pickup truck. Without further explanation, she hugged me hard in a way that only mothers could. April and Michelle drove up behind her, and I hung my head in shame and relief. They emerged from their cars, arms held wide with empathy, standing alongside the brick and mortar of my broken dream. I displayed the key for the last time, unlocking the coffee shop door. The four of us entered without words. Michelle and April approached the furniture, lifting chairs from their homes and art from the hooks.

As the space was cleared, Mom and I ripped the espresso machine from the water line, leaving a note of apology for our inaccurate measuring as the small trickle of water streamed down the wall. I worked without emotion, focused only on the task at hand. When the last remnant of the coffee shop was packed away, I left the key conspicuously on the counter and locked the door behind me. Wires hung sullenly from the walls where artwork once displayed their hopeful existence. When we stepped outside, my sisters and I hugged once more. They let me know they would take care of the rest. Dad was waiting at home and would store everything in their basement until I needed it again. I thanked them over and over until there was nothing left to say. Mom hoisted her small frame into the large truck and drove my belongings home. I lowered myself into my car, not knowing where I was going. Without looking back, I imagined the trail of dust leaving my back tires and settling onto the dissipation of my dreams.

Over the next three months, Ryan and I built a cave around us. He moved into an apartment with a friend of mine from college. I pretended to live with my sister while slowly trespassing my belongings into their space. Our eyes grew accustomed to the darkness of daily living. I found a job consulting for a company called "New Beginnings," laughing at the irony. Ryan began school for a degree in computer science, hoping to make enough money for us to find a place we could call our own. I spent my days working, cooking, and exercising, avoiding the ache of loss.

Ryan's parents chose to leave Pastor Bill's church shortly after Ryan and I were excommunicated. They asked us to join them at Ryan's sister's church. Jenny and her husband, Michael, were kind and inviting. They asked us to go to lunch with their friends after the services, and we were quickly made to feel welcome. It was a growing church in a small town, much like the one I grew up attending. When the pastor discovered Ryan's experience leading bands, he was asked to play guitar for their services. I remained a wallflower, guarded and dismissive. Women in small towns love to talk. I am good at listening, so I smiled and nodded along. The relationship worked. I began to lean into Ryan's family, and over the next year, they encouraged our relationship with every Sunday invitation. When Ryan and I were not playing house, going to school, or working, we spent time with his family. Mostly, his mom and I talked about nutrition, natural living, home remedies, and yoga. She was peculiar, warm, always welcoming, and loved Jesus. Her quiet strength resonated with my longing, and I drank it like a warm cup of tea.

As I brushed my teeth before bed one night after coming home from a family dinner, I paused and looked at Ryan.

"Are we going to keep doing this or actually get married?" I asked.

"Get married, of course," Ryan replied, putting his toothbrush down beside mine. "I just have to figure out how to make some more money."

"I have money," I said. "Not as much as I did before the coffee shop, but I can try and sell some of the stuff I have left over."

Ryan didn't answer but turned into the bedroom and flicked on the phone screen. Distracted by the glow, he thumbed through passively, ignoring my conversation.

Chapter 10

Four more months passed with no mention of commitment, just daily living in the gray. My boldness thickened over time.

"So, here's the thing," I said during another long Sunday drive to meet with his family. "I don't want to just live with you anymore if you cannot make a commitment to me. I need you to make a decision. You can marry me, or I can move out. Just let me know. I'm good either way. I can't keep pretending this is something that it isn't. And I really love your family, but they would be heartbroken if they knew we were hiding this way."

"I guess we're not having sex until you have a ring, huh?" he barked.

"Is that all you think about?" I scowled in his direction.

"Rings cost money. We'll figure it out, but we don't need to figure it out today. I don't know what you're so worried about. It's not like we're having sex. Isn't that your big hang-up?" Ryan sped through traffic as I stared out the window in silence.

"Look," Ryan said. "If you want to have a ring, you know what you want, so buy one."

"This isn't about a ring; this is about our relationship," I conceded.

"Let's get married then. I'm serious. Pick out a ring, and we will figure it out, okay?" Ryan looked over and smiled, both hands gripping the wheel.

The next day, I scoured online and purchased two rings. When the small brown package arrived in the mail, I handed it to Ryan unopened. "Here, now you have no excuses. When you are ready, you have our rings."

We were engaged by the end of the afternoon.

Now that the dream of owning a coffee shop was dead, I poured myself into planning our wedding. The edge of new romance had worn itself smooth. There were no piano serenades or afternoon trips to the beach. We felt responsible under the weight of our metal promise. Ryan began teaching himself coding to secure a computer software position, and I started a grueling exercise program in light of our bright future. The anticipation of a life together (minus a roommate) took on the shape of green bridesmaid dresses and well-frosted cakes. Ryan had nearly zero interest in wedding planning, besides what lingerie would be hiding underneath the eternity of creased satin. I assured him he would be able to find me eventually.

In trying to plan for friends to become bridesmaids, my search came up wanting. In the ebb and flow of new beginnings and moving, I had lost connection with my female relationships from school, work, and church. I called my sisters to once again come to my rescue and take me dress shopping. Having become well versed in church culture's expectation of modesty and women, I learned the art of avoidance, not wanting to wear anything that would bring unnecessary attention to my body. With every decision, I envisioned the eyes of each person in the room staring back at me. As I peered in the bridal store mirror, all I could think was: *I look like an oversized marshmallow. This is not me.* I took a shallow breath and succumbed to the "oohs" and "aahs" of the onlooking crowd. Michelle had tears in her eyes. I smiled. Cringing at the price tag but not wanting to try on another dress, I said yes.

A date was circled on the calendar for September. Save the dates were addressed to family members I had never met and a handful of friends we scrounged together. Our honeymoon to Mexico was agreed upon and booked before we had chosen a place for the ceremony. The resort held the promise I had waited so long to fulfill by consummating everything we had worked to achieve on our own. Dreams of parties, petit fours, parasols, and little girls in flowered dresses consumed my imagination. My aunt and uncle graciously offered their house to host our affair, and we made plans to set up tables and chairs on the newly finished landscape.

Ryan's dad built a canopy that would symbolize God's protection over our newly forged life together, our new home. I spent my free time creating handmade accents from cotton fabrics and ivy leaves. Dreaming up new ideas was a distraction from the brokenness of the coffee shop. I undertook a new origin, a new beginning, a new version of me.

Ryan's parents became our mentors, walking us through premarital counseling. We talked about how many kids we wanted to raise, gender roles, who would do the majority of the cleaning and cooking, and which one of us would work. We talked about marriage as if it were a well-designed program for living in every way, except for having sex. Sex was never mentioned. After six weeks of conversation, we received their seal of approval. In many ways, Ryan's parents reminded me of my own, with a more profound sense of connection and communication between them. Ryan's dad hugged me tightly, praising me with affection and affirmations. He greeted me with open arms and a big smile. The qualities I admired about my Dad rested in him as well. He was a hard-working man, always thinking about ways to provide for his family. Ryan's mom also reminded me, in a myriad of ways, of my own. She was gentle, kind, fiercely in love with the Bible, and knowledgeable about holistic medicines. I sensed she could be trusted with secrets, but I didn't dare share what lay behind the fig leaves of my shame for fear she would see me as impure.

The sun's rays cascaded across the wooden floor through the open slats of windows lining the entryway. Two of the girls I babysat were napping for the afternoon. I opened my laptop to look up the addresses of a few last relatives before putting the stack of wedding invitations in the mailbox. The wedding was four months away, and this felt like the last arduous task before we could relax into our celebration. I thoughtlessly clicked on social media, and at the top of the inbox, there was one unopened message with no subject line. Enjoying the moment of silence that filled the house, I took a deep breath and sighed it out. Opening the message, I scanned over the first few lines:

> I know that you don't know who I am. And this message is completely out of the blue, but you need to know something before you get married. I met Ryan in Panama City, at church summer camp, in July, last year, when he was in the praise and worship band. We flirted a bunch during camp, and since then, he has been cheating on you with me.

A ringing in my ears overtook the silence. *My face was on fire.* I could feel the carbon dioxide leaving my body with no oxygen returning. *Oh, God.* I forced my eyes to focus.

> It started off something really small. We were just friends, and we texted each other a lot. Then, all of a sudden, he was telling me how badly he wanted to kiss me, how amazing my skin was, and how beautiful I was . . . and I ate it all up. Next thing I knew, we were kissing . . . which, of course, led to other things.

The room is spinning. Oh, God. I'm going to throw up.

> After that, I started to really like him. I knew he had a girlfriend the entire time, but I always thought it was just a fling because that's how he portrayed it. I asked him if he was really in love a while back, and he told me he didn't know. So, I figured your relationship wasn't serious.

We're engaged. This can't be happening. Our relationship isn't serious? How much more serious can our relationship be?

> I have seen him a lot over this past year, and lately, it has gotten worse. I can't tell you how many times he has told me he needs to make love to me. At one point, neither of us could find a safe place to have sex without getting caught. He told me how he could rent a hotel room for us, so we could do it there. I am not one of those girls to go around and screw up people's relationships, but this whole

> thing happened. I'm trying to make things right now. This is the first time I have ever done anything like this in my entire life. I just kept hoping he would break up with you (and he made it sound like he was), but he never did. I moved and tried to forget about him because I knew what we were doing was sinful. But I went right back to him after a few months. While you guys have been engaged, he has continued to cheat on you repeatedly.

The tears scoured hot on my face, and I was breathless. I felt drunk and heavy, my body allowing gravity to pull me onto the cold, hard floor below. *I was drowning.*

> This message isn't something out of anger. I am telling you this because if I were in your shoes, I would want someone to tell me. I have wanted to send this message to you for a long time. I have prayed about it and feel that now is the time to tell you. I don't think you really know the person you're about to marry, and it would be unfair for you to get married and not know about all of this. I could actually care less about ever seeing Ryan again because, after this, I realized who he actually is as a person. I even asked him if we'd continue having sex once he got married. And his answer was, "Of course I would! Do you think I would make love to you and then drop you?! No way." This is coming from the man you're about to marry, and I don't think it's fair to you. I'm sure you are a wonderful person, and I am so sorry about all of this. I wish I had never even met him because, throughout all of this, I knew that I was hurting you in the process. I can't live in this sin any longer. I also asked Ryan, a long time ago, if he would ever tell you about me, and he said no. And I don't think it's right for you to get married to someone who you obviously don't know. Ryan might tell you that this is all untrue and I'm making this up. He will probably tell you I was the one who pursued him, and it's all my fault. He will deny the whole thing. But that's not the truth. I really did

like Ryan, a lot, actually, but he is not engaged to me. He is a very sweet guy, and if you two get married, I really do wish the best for both of you. I'm sure that doesn't mean anything to you, though. I'm sure you won't respond to this, but you need to know the truth. I'm sorry again for everything.

I wept silently, trying not to wake the sleeping girls. Holding myself up with one hand on the hardwood floor, the rest of my body dropped from the couch. My neck craned upward, and an audible gasp filled the empty space. I was sweating; my body was cold and clammy. I wiped my eyes continually, trying to make the words disappear. I could not push the unread button and make everything untrue.

My fingers were numb as I grasped the phone to dial Ryan's number. His voicemail picked up, and at the sound of his voice, I hung up quickly. Then, I redialed, becoming manic. The phone rang two more times before he picked up.

"Hey!" he answered.

"Who is Marcie?" I asked.

"What?" Ryan replied.

"Who . . . is . . . Marcie?" I repeated.

"I don't know anyone named Marcie," he responded.

"I just received an email from a girl named Marcie. She says she knows you," my words exited with an eerie calm.

There was a hesitation from the receiver, and I grabbed the back of my neck. My skin felt detached from the rest of my body.

"Christine, what are you talking about?" Ryan asked.

"Just be honest with me, Ryan. Tell me who Marcie is," I was strained underneath the current of fear.

"Oh, gosh, are you talking about that senior girl?" Suddenly, there was an epiphany. "You remember how I worked that summer camp last year? She was the drummer in our band. I thought she had feelings for me, but it was like some high school crush. It was nothing serious, so I didn't even know who you were talking about." Ryan paused.

"Is there anything else?" I asked, trying to control my tone.

"I never wanted you to worry about it. That's why I didn't tell you. It was nothing. She liked me. I told her that I had a girlfriend, and that was it. There is nothing to worry about. Trust me," Ryan's voice was smooth with reassurance.

"I can do that, Ryan. But we need to talk about this more. She made it sound like things were way more serious between you. Why would she lie about it? Anyway, I'm just really confused right now," I looked down at the stack of invitations lying on the couch beside me, waiting to be sent.

"I'm sorry. I can't talk now, though. I'm at work, and I need to go. We'll talk tonight, okay?" The phone clicked in my ear.

"Okay," I said into the nothingness.

I fell onto my knees into a child's pose, this time defeated. *Oh, God.* I cried out, waiting to gain clarity. I was surrounded by a warm sensation cascading over my body, like being at the ocean, calmed by the magnitude of waves and tenderly kissed by the sun. There was a feeling of a hand gently placed on my back, the weight sinking me deeper. I shut my eyes tight. I felt as if I were dying, but there was nothing but peace to fall into. I stretched my hands out, palms down, and let go.

The afternoon blurred into the evening as I drove to the Robinson's house for my next babysitting job. Susan and Josh were going out to dinner, and I was watching their two dark-haired girls. Kyla was playing with play dough when I stumbled through the door. Meira was still asleep from her afternoon nap. Susan looked at me and immediately asked me if there was something wrong. I held back tears and nodded yes. She stood from her kitchen table and swept me into her bedroom, where I collapsed onto the floor. Susan sat beside me and asked if I wanted to talk. I cracked under the weight. I presented both sides of the story, trying to withhold any details that would make my fiancé look poorly in her eyes.

She listened patiently until I was finished and said without hesitation, "What will you do if it's true?"

I wept at the thought. Susan placed her mother's arms around me, and I sobbed heavily into her shoulder. The smell of lavender enveloped my senses, and I breathed her in.

"I'm so sorry, honey," she whispered.

"I forwarded Marcie's message to Ryan but have not heard from him since we talked on the phone. That was four hours ago," I looked up at her and shook my head slowly, letting the reality swirl around to saturate my thoughts.

It was late when Susan and Josh arrived home from their date. With no word from Ryan, I resolved to learn the truth. Driving to his apartment instead of Michelle's place, where I had stayed since the engagement, I found my key and opened the door. Ryan looked surprised, wide-eyed, and panicked. He met me at the door where I stood, and hours' worth of internal toil spilled out.

Frustrated and confused, I yelled, "You've been home this whole time?"

"Yeah, I'm sorry. I needed some time to think," Ryan replied. He moved in closer.

"How could you not call me? I need some reassurance from you, Ryan! You have to tell me what is going on," I said sternly, not taking my gaze away from his. I wanted to hold his truth. I wanted him to see my desperation and fear like a wounded animal awaiting judgment.

He was silent. The dark of Ryan's hair electrified the blue in his eyes as he looked up at me. His thin lips remained closed, unwilling to soothe the thousand shadows that chased behind the truth. My mind reeled through each possibility.

"Is it true?" I finally asked.

Ryan took a step closer without a word.

"Just tell me the truth, Ryan. What she said in that letter . . . is it true?"

He dropped to his knees before me and placed his head in his hands.

I recoiled into the wall, staring at his body limp beneath me. I was towering over him with palpable silence between us.

We remained in the tension until the truth prevailed. "Yes."

My jaw clenched, eyes steady on the curve of his back. My shoulder pulsed, radiating numbing pain down toward my fingers.

"All of it?" I continued in a low tone.

He shook his head slowly, "Yes. All of it."

My face turned to stone as my legs lost the ground beneath

me. I slid my back down the smooth wall to hold whatever form of me was left. With covered faces, we both wept in our own worlds. Ryan reached his arm out to touch mine, and I jerked away, letting it fall beside him. There was no comfort to offer. None to receive. No words were spoken between us. Time and circumstance magnified the tiredness of my frame, and I crawled my way to the nearest chair, where I cried until my eyes closed.

    I woke to an empty room, remembering Ryan had been seated on the couch beside me when I fell asleep. There was a sharp pain behind my right eye, and I focused on the coffee table before me, bringing reality back into sight. My eyes focused on a knife resting on an unfinished project of Ryan's roommate. I picked it up and ran my finger along the slanted blade, hoping for the sharp edge to pierce my skin enough to awaken my nerve endings. *Why live if you already feel nothing? Have nothing?* It took a few dead moments before scaring myself back to my senses. I put the knife down in the precise place it had been left, and hoisting my weight from the chair, I walked into the kitchen. There was a bottle of rum on the blue-flecked countertop. I opened it and swallowed a mouthful, wincing. Then, I choked down two more.

    Fumbling through the cabinets, I took out a large black trash bag and began my expedition. Walking to the bookcase, I pulled Chesterton and Lewis from their orphanage and tossed them into the open bag. Two shelves below, I spotted a book of photos I had compiled for our year anniversary of dating. Scanning through the flimsy pages of memories, I landed on a photo where dotted faces huddled together. It was the summer camp from last year. Somewhere in that sea of faces was Marcie. She was smiling back, unknowingly tearing apart the one chance I felt I had to rebuild my life on something I thought worthy of calling love. I lingered over each face, imagining Ryan's words to the girl in the photo. Eight months of hushed conversations and uninhibited bodies while I mindlessly picked out a white dress to wear down the aisle.

    With all of the mistakes I had chosen for myself and unwise decisions met with eternal consequences, the one vow I kept was to never have sex with anyone other than my husband.

There, in that picture, the face of every female mocked me. What an idiot.

When Ryan showed his face through the door, I had finished off a quarter-liter of rum and packed all my belongings. The charming smile he once possessed had taken the shape of a joker. His thin long nose pointed out above his even thinner upper lip. When I told him that I'd collected all of my belongings to leave, Ryan asked me to stay for a few minutes. I sat down and listened to a well-scripted apology and a thorough explanation of why and how this would never happen again. Examining the crime scene, I mentally deliberated the other list of options. Susan's question pulsed in my ears, *what if it's true?* The alternative to staying is an empty page. The last two days had been a succession of long pauses, and I was terrified. The fear of loneliness was a powerful motivator.

"If we are going to work through this, you must tell your parents," I conceded.

Ryan hesitantly agreed. We drove the hour's drive through the mountains to Ryan's family log cabin in silence. By the time we arrived, I was sober, and neither one of us was willing to say more than what had already been divulged. Ryan's dad was waiting in the driveway when we pulled up. He opened my door and hugged me tightly, the familiarity of his soft flannel shirt against my face. Ryan's father pushed open the front door for me to go ahead, and their golden lab came bounding in to greet me. I put my hand down methodically, and she nudged the door closed behind us. Trained loyalty. People live and die for that conditioned response to love.

It took seven minutes for Ryan to make his confession. "We're going to try and make it work, though," he said, glancing at me for reassurance. We just wanted to tell you guys so that you know," he finished his sentence without emotion.

Ryan's parents counseled us through what the next steps would look like should we choose to stay engaged. They encouraged me not to talk to anyone else about what had happened and to continue planning our wedding.

"We understand," they said almost in unison.

Ryan's mom interjected, "You know, Ryan's dad and I

broke up for a short time before we got married. I would be willing to share with you more about it if you think it would be helpful."

I didn't want to hear about anyone else's heartache. Mine was sufficient for the time. There were no more tears left within me, and dehydration, at some point, took over. *Am I becoming so isolated in planning our future that I fail to see what is happening in the very bed I sleep in at night?* We were building a house of cards on the sand, but I was determined to make it work. *That's what love does, right? It stays, even when everything is falling apart.*

In the month leading up to our wedding, my nightmares became pervasive. I awoke not remembering the details, but a distinct feeling of panic created shallow breaths as I regained a footing in reality. Examining the sheets torn from the corners of the bed and drenched in sweat, I called my counselor. We sat together in the darkness of the unknown, bringing pieces of my story to light. Julie and I discussed childhood feelings of abandonment and ongoing disordered eating patterns. We also unearthed my inability to name the experiences with Alex and Derek as "sexual abuse." We began to unravel the history of lies I had carried with me over time. My worth was interwoven with my ability to be loved, which, in my mind, could only be earned. Revisiting my childhood, Julie connected the relationship to my earthly Dad with the perception I projected on God, thereby holding men hostage to a responsibility to fill that void of love I desired to hold. By continuing to walk toward marriage, I placed Ryan in the gap.

The day after Ryan confessed to his parents, I booked an appointment with Julie. She listened with intent and then spent time praying for guidance from the Holy Spirit. It felt like a gift.

"It sounds like you've made the decision to stay and love this man despite his confessed sin," she affirmed. "That takes strength."

I wanted to be strong. I listed the thousand sins I had made in my life and justified the one time I had been wronged by Ryan. The scale tipped in his favor.

After praying together, I left her office feeling more certain than the day before. *I can make this work. No one has to know what Ryan did. I just have to keep breathing. Keep moving forward.* I thought of the countless nights Mom spent on the couch while Dad raged. She chose to stay. I would, too.

Down the hallway in the church where Julie and I met, there was a midday service humming in the sanctuary. I slipped into the quiet space and found a chair near the back of the room. The seats were spotted with only a few members who had snuck away from the monotony of their workday to find reprieve in the words spoken and songs sung. My mind was a water mill, picking up recycled thoughts and dumping them into the stream of consciousness. When it was time to stand for communion, I thought about how naïve I was as a young child. Walking down the aisle in a white dress and veil for my first communion in the Catholic Church, I had no idea the road would lead to this place, this church, or these people whom I didn't know. However, I felt the ease to shuffle into and out of their service just to feel nourished by something good.

As I walked to the communion table, tears stained my face. The young girl in the white dress was still me. *I can't walk down that aisle with Ryan. I have to believe there is something better than this, someone better. I have to believe I am something more.*

"This is the body of Christ, broken for you."

"This is the blood of Christ, shed for you."

I took the bread and wine, body and blood, and tasted redemption. I swallowed it down, wanting it to take hold of my insides.

A woman behind me with dark hair and freckled skin placed her hand on my shoulder as we returned to our seats.

"Are you okay?" she whispered from behind me.

I shook my head yes and almost smiled.

When the service ended, I remained transfixed on the large crucifix hung high above the simple stage. A warm hand reached around my shoulder and remained. I recounted the last two days to the pastor who sat beside me.

He paused but was unwavering in his conviction. "Marriage is fundamentally about trust. This man to whom you are engaged has deeply broken any foundation of trust that could be laid for you both moving forward. You are engaged, not married. There is no obligation for you to stay if that is not what you really want."

I nodded in agreement for the first time, soaking in truth.

"Your tendency will be to isolate yourself, but I want to encourage you to lean into the community around you. There are good and trusted people around. We are all here for you through this. I'm so sorry." The pastor finished speaking and put an affirming hand on my shoulder. I had no reason to trust this man other than to acknowledge faith is a risk to believe in something bigger than ourselves.

In a moment of clarity, the tiredness and ache of tears disintegrated into a peace that truly surpassed any understanding. I walked into the space, willing myself to seal the cracks of a broken relationship, no matter the damage it did to my soul. I left, patching the broken dishes with gold, claiming sincerity. I walked out of the sanctuary with bold confidence in a future hope. *A blank page does not mean I have nothing but that I have everything left in me to begin my story.*

I smiled wide as a monologue began taking form in my mind. Clearing it away with a breath, I prayed fervently and honestly for the first time in years, "Holy Spirit, just give me the strength I need to say what I need to say."

Ryan was alone in the apartment. He was surprised to see me when I came in the front door. He meandered over slowly, uncomfortably. I smiled reassuringly.

"Ryan," I took in a deep breath before continuing. "I love you. And, because I love you, I cannot stay with you."

I paused to let the reality sink into my ears, and his.

"I want the best for you, and I do not believe this is what is best. You need community. You need to learn to love people around you. You need to learn to receive grace without judgment and to be honest with yourself and with others. I need time to heal, and I need that to be outside of our relationship."

Ryan sat down on the floor cross-legged in front of my feet. I knelt down and wrapped my arms around him.

"I've really messed up," he cried. "Please don't leave me."

"I'm sorry, Ryan. I can't do this anymore. I believe God has something better for you, for us both," I finished.

Standing up with a confidence that could not be mustered, only received, I pulled the apartment key off of my key ring and placed it gently onto the counter. I slid the ring from my finger and set it beside the key. Engraved is one word: charity. *If we gain the whole world and have not love, we have nothing.*[8]

"Goodbye, Ryan," I whispered before closing the door.

He did not look up from where he was seated on the floor.

As I drove away, a shift happened in my soul. The air was light; my shoulders felt unfettered from the weight. A powerful calm sat in the base of my belly, like the ocean after a night storm. Without knowing where to drive, I harbored at Susan's. She made a bed for me in their basement, and I lay on the top of the comforter, staring at the popcorn ceiling. In the emptiness of my body, I felt the subtle beating of my heart against my ribs. I ran my fingers against the skin of my belly, up to my chest, trying to contain the sound. The rise of breath filled me and sank lower than before. Entitlement of this breath, this beat, this life, struck a pain into my side. I placed my hands alongside my weary legs, palms up, ready to receive. *Nothing is given that has not first been received.*[9] In the silence, the rhythm grew louder. *Inhale. Exhale.* With each breath, I felt cleansed from within. We can be reborn as many times as it takes to become fully alive to ourselves.

Chapter 11

Susan and her family spent a week out of town, so I occupied the space in their absence. Susan left a bottle of wine, a bar of dark chocolate, and a lavender bubble bath on the nightstand beside their oversized bed. I slept in, drank wine, ate chocolate, and bathed in lavender. Then, I rinsed and repeated the homeopathy for seven consecutive days. When their family arrived home, I asked Susan and Josh if I could stay with them until I was ready to embrace the changes needed for me to move forward. They agreed, and I began to feel, in many ways, adopted into their family.

It had been almost a year since I began watching Kyla and her baby sister, Meira. Kyla was approaching four years old and had one long, dark, curly strand of hair hanging down from the rest. We called it her rat curl. Kyla was an inquisitive and bright-eyed child, imaginative and free-spirited. She and I spent our days singing loudly on car rides, leapfrogging from ballet lessons to art class to the playground. I sang her a song, rubbing her back as the nighttime ritual commenced. She turned to me and asked, "Ms. Christine, how can Jesus be in my heart and all around us at the same time?"

I whispered a grown-up-sounding response, lying beside her in a toddler-sized bed. As I closed my eyes, I understood Christ's sacrifice for His children in a way that I never knew before. For the first time, I felt a love so immense that it could lay down itself for another. Jake would not offer that within the whims of our youthful passions. Derek, so absorbed and wounded, could not bear to look past his own soul in order to save another. Ryan had never received the freedom and power of grace to extend beyond his ego. And all this time, I believed love could be controlled and possessed, allowing false promises and hollow words to seal the cracks of my wounds.

  The prayer of Saint Francis trickled down into my mouth and over my tongue as I sang it over the sleeping child, as I sang it over myself.

Lord, make me an instrument of peace;
Where there is hate, let me sow love;
Where there is hurt, let me bring your healing;

> *Make of me, Your hands and feet.*
> *I want to be to the people around me*
> *What you want to be to the people around me*

It's in the loving we find love.

> *For it is in giving that we receive;*
> *In the dying, we are found.*[10]

  I committed to stop recycling the same air in my lungs, repeating the same dizzying cycles. After a week of complete isolation, I heeded the pastor's advice and chose to take the first opportunity to find a wider community, signing up for a church softball league. Driving to the log cabin, I hugged Mom and Dad before Mom pointed me to the basement, where I surveyed the landscape of cardboard boxes. I found a large box shoved in the corner and tore the flaps apart. Inside, a tattered softball glove hid beneath a score of academic certificates and awkward school photos. I flipped through them quickly, smiling at the many haircuts I had endured. I turned the leather over in my hand to find large block letters spelling out my name C-H-R-I-S-T-I-N-E. I stepped into the reality of my given name like an old familiar glove.

  On the first day of softball practice, I called a friend, Jen, from church. "I wish you'd come with me," I whined.

  "Girl, I would love it if I had time to do that, but this new nursing job is crazy," She laughed. "You can do this," she encouraged. "Just remember who you are."

  "Yeah, remind me who that is again," I halfway joked.

"You're Christine. You've got this." Jen's confidence resounded. "Call me when you're done."

I pulled out a pair of cheerleading shorts buried in my drawer. For a moment, time was suspended, and I began to feel the same gnawing accusation of shame rise up within me. My fingers began to tingle. I shook Alex's memory from my attention, inhaled deeply, and grounded my reality back to the present moment.

"I am Christine," I whispered under my breath as a reminder. I pull the elastic-waisted shorts up over each leg. Looking down at the woman I had become, I wondered if I would ever release the little girl trapped inside. Walking slowly upstairs from my room in the basement, I hugged Kyla and Meira and waved goodbye before closing the door gently. Arriving at the park early, as introverts do, I parked the car and waited. I sat in my conspicuously gold-colored car and closed my eyes, hands still firmly grasping the steering wheel.

Deep breath. I can do this. Inhale. Exhale.

As people started to trickle out to the field, I turned to the passenger seat to grab my glove before opening the driver's side door. There were two fields dotted with different colored jerseys. I took another quick breath and proceeded down the middle lane, sparse with grass, until I reached the side where I matched the blue shirts to my own. The coach from the opposing team was a few feet away, all in black. He was dark and tall. He held a blonde child by her hands and spun her dizzy with laughter before setting her back onto her feet.

That is your husband.

The voice came so sure and steady in my mind that my body responded with a pause. It was the same one I heard all those years ago that night in bed. The unmistakable Voice. I looked around to make sure I was alone in my thoughts and laughed aloud. I responded to the ludicrous announcement by reassuring myself that the man twirling this little girl in front of me was indeed someone incredibly attractive, yet he would have no committed lifetime spent beside me. I was convinced I had been created for a life of celibacy.

I spoke with Jen as I drove him from softball practice. "So, was it as terrifying as you thought it would be?"

"Jen, there was this guy . . . " I could not formulate the sentence completely.

I looked down at the empty space where my purity ring, then the engagement ring, had wrapped around my finger. A deep sense of pride had been grabbed from my hand after the cancellation of our wedding. The pain of explaining Ryan's unfaithfulness only furthered the embarrassment. I kept silent, mostly, except for Susan and Jen, who held my pain without diminishing questions like, "How did you not know?" After the devastation, Ryan and I agreed to keep attending the same church on the understanding we would attend separate services.

"What guy?" She responded inquisitively.

"It's nothing. I don't know. I have seen him around the church before. Just curious who he is." I downplayed my curiosity. Jen moved on, "The church is holding a restoration workshop this weekend, and I really can't go alone." She begged, "Please come with me."

"You know I can't go, Jen. It's only been two weeks since I broke off the engagement, and I remember telling Ryan that he should go to that workshop. I just can't see him. It's too soon."

"I understand. Just please consider it. I think it would be good for you, too. I'll be there with you, so even if we see him, we can just pretend he isn't there," she stated nonchalantly.

"Yeah, I wish it were that simple," I laughed. I ended the conversation with the offer to consider the possibility.

I was on my way home from work that Friday evening when Jen called again.

"The workshop is tomorrow morning. I really don't want to go alone. I promise that if Ryan shows up, we can leave." She was desperate.

"I can't see him, Jen. It wouldn't be fair to him, and I just don't think I can hold myself together if I do," I admitted.

"I understand, but like I said, if he's there, we can go. No harm in trying, right?" she pushed.

"I'll go for you, but if his car is in the parking lot, we turn around. Promise?" I complied.

"Promise," she committed.

The next morning, I made sure to wear heels. The power trip was real. Coating my eyelashes once more with mascara, I raced out the door. I was grateful the church had good coffee, and I reasoned that if that were all I got out of this day, it would have at least started well. Jen met me in the parking lot of the church, spaces dotted with cars that did not resemble Ryan's car. We waited together to see if he arrived, but ten minutes after the workshop began, he was still nowhere to be seen. Feeling safe, we entered the sanctuary, where men and women of all ages gathered together to pray. Jen grabbed my hand, and we found seats tucked in the corner of the sanctuary. I gave her a raised eyebrow and a tight-lipped grin to let her know that everything was seemingly in our favor.

My counselor, Julie, was one of the speakers. She displayed a calm disposition and quiet tone. We reflected on our families of origin and honest relationships with God. It felt good to be stretched, to remember, and to forgive. During our break for lunch, Jen and I decided to walk to the grocery store. My shoes wore at my heels, peeling back layers of skin on the back of my ankles. As we returned to the cafe inside the church to eat, beads of sweat began to form at my temples. Seated in a bistro chair, we unpacked our array of food. Using my left foot, I pulled the strap off the back of my opposite shoe for some relief. I had just dipped a carrot into the vat of hummus when I glanced up to see the guy from softball practice standing at the coffee bar.

I leaned into Jen and whispered, "That's the guy I told you about from the softball field. I think his name is Kyle."

"Who?" she turned to look.

I slapped her arm playfully, "Don't turn around. We met like four years ago. He'd never remember me."

In college, my friends and I signed up for a Christmas dinner downtown. There was a homeless ministry that operated out of the church, and it was a way for us to get involved. I volunteered to pray with whomever wanted prayer while my friends joined the carol singers. Before we met up to leave, I was waiting in line to get food when Kyle turned around in the line in front of me. His guitar was strapped around a maroon leather jacket, and I remember thinking how odd it was that my grandma had just given me a leather jacket the same color. Kyle was playing "Kiss Me" by Sixpence None The Richer. I laughed and said aloud, "Well, you're presumptuous." He returned laughter and asked if he could walk my friends and me to our car.

"He's hot," Jen laughed, returning to our lunch.

"I just want him to stay far away," I said jokingly. "If he never speaks, then he can never disappoint me. He'll always be this far-off beacon of hope that not all men are terrible."

Jen grinned.

"Hey, I didn't know you were bringing salad for everyone. I wouldn't have eaten so many donuts," a voice interjected.

I looked up, my hand still halfway into the hummus container. Kyle was standing at our table, smiling. His brown eyes caught me off guard. I tried to think of something witty in response, but my brain slowed. I found myself unable to speak. Jen laughed, high-pitched and robust. She slapped her knee with fervent sarcasm.

"Hey, I'm Kevin." He stuck his hand out in Jen's direction, and my eyes widened. She caught my glance and held back the laughter in her throat. Kyle had actually been Kevin this whole time.

Jen jumped headlong into the conversation and naturally commanded her words, but Kevin's eyes never left mine. I stood from the chair, readjusted the strap on the back of my shoes, and walked toward the coffee. Kevin followed, waiting for me to refill my coffee cup.

"I haven't seen you around church lately," Kevin interjected.

"I, uh, I've been attending the night service," I replied.

"Oh, that makes sense. I volunteer in the morning, teaching the 4th and 5th grade classes. We've just missed each other," he eyed the coffee, slowly moving to the brim of the paper cup.

Now, standing in front of him, all of these years later, I begged for the return of time. Somehow, if I could just freeze-frame that moment in space four years ago, there would be no wasted time or broken engagements. No wounded hearts or shattered expectations. Everything might just be, well, the way it was intended. Not being one of the romantic notions of princes on white horses, my cynicism quickly gave way to the reality that the curse had been cast. Kevin *had* spoken. He was no longer an imaginary hero, void of flaws or an Achilles heel. We talked briefly over coffee, waiting for the next session to begin. He told me he was a middle school teacher, owned a beloved dog named Psyche, and was in the process of renovating a house nearby. Kevin lived a seemingly normal existence. A broken engagement, living in a basement, and still transitioning jobs, I felt like a mess in his presence.

I asked bluntly, "You seem so normal. Why aren't you married by now?"

Caught off guard by the boldness of my remark, yet still quick to answer, "I just haven't found someone I can see myself spending the rest of my life with yet."

I held my heart in a white paper cup filled with coffee, and my hands trembled. *I have nothing left to give, so how could he ask for anything?* He didn't. He gave only a smile and a gesture of pause to look at me long and lovingly. *I felt wanted.* The thought bubbled up to the surface, and I rationalized the sentiment back down to the bottom of the ocean. No one chooses a leaking cup to drink from. I was empty. I turned back toward Jen's warmth, her familiarity, and our uneaten lunch. Without a word, her eyes said everything my brain was working through, and I breathed in the reality that this could be something real.

The last session began. The blur of my conversation with Kevin and the intensity of desire and longing bled into every sentence spoken from the stage. My ears tuned in and out as I tried to focus. Emotion defied every logical thought. In my brokenness, I felt the pressure of being reshaped clay. The scraping away of impurity, balancing myself onto the Potter's wheel, with one foot on and the other flailing alongside. I gave in to allowing myself to feel the weight of the emotion, the betrayal, the broken engagement, and the abuse that still pulsed through my body when a person stood behind me. I wanted to be safe, whole, and desirous. I wanted to believe that what had shaped me did not define me. I was breathing deep, softening beneath the gentle push and pull.

As the workshop ended, Kevin stood before us, strumming the same guitar from years prior, but it was a different song. He led the sanctuary in song, declaring that our lives, when placed in the hands of Christ, become new. We become new. Christ comes in and makes way for us to do anything, to move forward, and to live. Truly live. I sang the words over my soul, desperate for them to take hold. My mind replayed the events of my life like a film reel, the pain and beauty that led me into this refuge. My hands were extended, palms up, ready again to receive. Maybe we must come empty to receive love, to give love. Maybe I could become something lovely, something lovable, by being loved. Moreover, maybe I had to choose that I am already loved by Someone far greater than those clothed in skin. I consider marriage a picture of God's great love for His bride. We're a battered and bruised body of believers, and Jesus says *come be my bride. You are already loved.*[11] Those words seeped into the hidden spaces where my chest still ached, and my shoulder throbbed. The unspoken world of those who feel like each day simply exists but not truly living.

Lovable.

My Beloved. Be Loved. Be Love. Be.

My breath began to steady in its rhythm as my diaphragm engaged each word. The Holy Spirit moved through the space of my body.

As I began to find what it truly means to be saved by Love and what it means to believe that I am loved and am love, the lie began to dim. I received the truth on offer and rewrote the narrative. These words hold power and shape our DNA. "Unlovable" becomes "unbelievably loved." "Beloved." I sat under the truth of those words and let them rewrite my name, my identity. One glorious defeat of the enemy led me to reclaim the abundant life. I began to accept that salvation is not left for the other side of eternity, for a select few Christians, or for those who seemingly have it all together. It is the *reason* Jesus came in a form we can touch!

There is attainable joy within reach, an identity that, when spoken over us by Christ, will dispel unthinkable pain, and a peace that comes from knowing and walking with a wounded Savior. Because it is by His stripes we are healed, we are invited into His suffering so we may also share in His glory. The reason is summed up in one word: Love.

There *is* a journey that leads to wholeness and a sense of sustained peace in the process when we show up. It is not enough to bypass the cross and dance on the other side of the resurrection. We must sit in the darkness of unknowing and allow ourselves to feel it all. We must let the pain move through us into spaces of greater freedom. It is a walk in the garden, feet darkened with soil, hands pressed into clay. Joy is found through knowing the suffering is finished instead of continuing to invite it back into life.
I opened the door to step into freedom far beyond the confines of the rules and rituals of those in power. I had wanted for so long to proudly display my all-A Honor Roll and receive, "Well done." Instead, I was invited to show my true self with risky vulnerability and receive, "I love you; come home." It hurt like hell.

Julie shared an ancient practice called breath prayer in which each inhale and exhale is shaped by the thought, intention, and words desired to commune with Father, Son, and Spirit. I learned to breathe again, each inhale and exhale the very life, the very breath, the very name of YHWH. God breathed into the clay and dry bones to whisper, "Come alive." Inhale. Yah. Exhale. Weh. This gasping of breath is a grasping for the Eternal. My breath is the presence of the Spirit of God, animating my limbs to move, enjoy, create, and dance. It is my practice and my prayer. This Spirit, my very breath, carried me through every severed relationship and brought me back home to myself.

I got into the car and pulled away from the workshop, dialing Jen's number.

"Jen, I can't stop thinking about him. Please just tell me to stop. Tell me it isn't right. It's too soon. It's not good. Anything. Tell me it isn't worth it to try and love again. I can't go through this again only to be hurt." I pleaded with her to give me a reason not to trust myself.

"Christine, I know this will sound crazy, but I can't tell you that. You should be cautious, but it's worth giving this a chance."

She told me she was with me and hung up the phone.

    Back home, in my tiny basement apartment, I got onto my yoga mat and breathed. Face buried in the ground, I extended my hands. Instead of defeat, it was a posture of surrender—an active letting go of believing I was unworthy of love. I breathed in and out, God, knowing each breath is another grace of being alive. It is my only hope, my only prayer. God, closer than my very breath.

Chapter 12

The day Kevin and I got married, we met in a field of waist-high grass. I pulled the pleats of my dress up to my knees as I jumped over the conjoined trains standing still on the tracks. His tall, slender back stood like a wall before me, an X marked by suspenders. Not everyone received the opportunity to redeem relationships and time. The weight of glory sat heavy on my breast. I opened the invitation left on my pillow so long ago, hearing the words repeatedly in my mind. *Christine, You are My Beloved.* Kevin turned to me, seeing me as his soon-to-be wife for the first time. Eyes alight, Kevin's arms wrapped around my waist as he pulled me close into the harbor of his safe arms. Time slowed as we acknowledged our inability to grasp this eternal moment.

Kevin leaned close to pray, voice hushed, "God, thank you for this woman to call my own. Thank you that she is Yours first, and this is just the beginning of our story together."

I am his, and he is mine. There is no beginning or end to where our stories intertwine. We basked in the sunlight, feeling the suspension of dusk and dawn.

Kevin and I grasped a cluster of white balloons, each containing a memory of our past. We scribbled confessions of regret and tied them onto the end of each balloon. Together, we held hands and released the balloons one by one, staring up into the vast sky until they drifted out of sight.

"And the two will become one flesh,"[12] the provocative unveiling of the Holy Spirit as our souls collided that day in April. Kevin and I stood hand in hand, my beloved and I, and we consecrated our marriage. The complexity and simplicity of a relationship are recreated—made new. Whatever the words or bread broken or glasses cheered, I saw glimpses of the unity between Father, Son, and Holy Spirit pour into our newly vowed lives. On the night of our wedding, we stood naked and unashamed before one another. Our minds, hearts, and bodies are given without restraint. It is a sealed covenant.

I wanted to believe that in that one act, the shame of sin and abuse would be licked clean by our prayers. Forgiveness would be sought, wounds salved, and we would begin our story as a new family. And yet, in my humanity, I was unfamiliar with freedom, so I found new spaces to hide. Kevin and I carried into our marriage old suitcases, tattered at the seams, worn down from the years we had dragged them behind us. Relationships bent and broken, we both shared places in our lives where undue affection is given to those less than worthy of our attention. We spent our early days unpacking the details of our past relationships, untangling the mess of our brokenness. Each untold story led to another, finding ease with each piece taken into the light of Love. The Light exposes our darkness, each missed target dimly lit within the presence of Christ. In the sharing, we moved closer to one another, trusting the safety of attachment. Fear holds no sway in the permission to be fully known and loved, but the courage to receive such permission takes a lifetime.

Healing is a process. My body ached with the newness of safety while trauma remained stored in my bones. No longer using distraction, food, and alcohol to numb the pain, I began to feel it all. Spending days in childhood learning to protect myself from being hurt, I involuntarily cringed beneath the tenderness of Kevin's touch. We lay in bed most nights, and I felt paralyzed by both desire and distance. I longed for him to pull me into the safety of his embrace, but when he did, I turned to stone. Tears ran heavily, and I could not speak. He pushed away, scared he was hurting me. I could not verbally respond, only shake my head 'yes' or 'no.' I was silenced by unspoken harm. What was once safe and beautiful intimacy turned into suffocating memories. As Kevin placed his hand gently on my knee, I felt the shame and guilt of my past resurface. I could not shake my demons, and they were unwilling to let me go. The closer Kevin and I moved toward vulnerable intimacy, the more my body cried out. I shook uncontrollably under his touch until he wrapped his arms around me tightly. The rise and fall of his chest taught me again how to breathe. On other days, the pain moved through my body, reminding me of all the ways I was not safe. For the first six months of our marriage, I ended most days crying on the closet floor.

Marriage felt like a lie. Something was missing from the forgiveness I spoke in our vows. Past sins paraded into our marriage and threatened to beckon me back into the self-made prison of guilt and shame. I lay in bed at night, torn by thoughts of my past relationships and scars. My reckless past decisions left me feeling empty in this waste of covenant life.

"Why do I continue to suffer for the sins committed by others?" I whispered after a night of tormented thoughts.

"I don't know what you mean," Kevin responded. I opened my heart and hands to Kevin in marriage but chose to shut off the parts of myself that were still too embarrassed and ashamed to use words like "abuse," much less knowing how to move forward in light of that truth.

Before I could finish my thought, I broke. Images of the cross filled my mind. My sin. Christ's holy hands. Redemption. Jesus chose out of His great love to endure the cross for the sins of humanity. To reclaim the broken places. To rename my identity despite my wrongdoings. I wept uncontrollably. I no longer had to carry the weight of this sin. Within this new marriage was a choice to love and experience forgiveness and freedom. It is finished, yet I keep searching for more nails.

Kevin turned toward me, his face close enough to feel a warm breath on my forehead. "I don't know what you're going through. I want to help you, but I cannot do anything unless you let me know what is happening. I know you've had some hard times in the past, but I love you. And that isn't changing. Whatever it is, you don't have to carry it alone anymore. I'm here. I am not afraid of your brokenness. My love is not fragile," he whispered as we drifted into rest.

After months of staying hidden, I began to feel safe enough to share, dipping my toe into the pool of exposure.

Vulnerability is a terrifying risk. I divulged my pain slowly, opening up about my past—the abuse and abandonment. Kevin remained anchored, unwavering in my sea of grief. I was refreshed in his presence. I let him into a deeper knowing and relinquished the expectation for him to fix me or make me whole. On Thursday nights, I took my computer into an empty house room, unrolled my yoga mat, and sat on the ground. I showed up as simply and honestly as possible and asked the Holy Spirit to give me only what I could hold for one day. I was ready to heal. I closed my eyes and waited, allowing my breath to relax. Each memory was a fresh pain as if it was happening all over again in the present. I wanted to run away, but I waited, allowing the ache to surface instead of pressing it down. I breathed into the sensation, noting where it manifested in my body. The pain began to shift, sometimes in the form of movement, releasing the energy and tension until it was no longer present. Other times, I lay still, allowing the tears to baptize me as I released deeper into surrender. Each time I entered the sacred space, I asked God to show me where Love is when I am alone, abused, and depressed. My perspective shifted as I saw the story through God's eyes or the eyes of myself, now grown, compassionately witnessing the little girl I still carried around with me.

 Slowly, painfully, I peeled back the layers of forgiveness starting in my mind, letting it trickle down toward my heart and into my hands. Some days, I wrote. On other days, I sat quietly, extending forgiveness over myself, over those who had hurt me, and those whom I had hurt. Surrender was an active rebellion to no longer allow the weight of the past to hold sway over my marriage, over my identity, and over my view of the world as anything but good.

 Like a broken piece of pottery, I laid myself down on the yoga mat and allowed the radical love of God to seal each cracked fragment with gold, similar to the Japanese art of Kintsugi. In the repair process, wounds became beautiful scars, markers of my history instead of excuses to hide. I began to see the truest parts of myself emerge in my belovedness. Little joys returned as I embraced the woman I was before I fell into the lie of being unlovable. I began to sing again, to dance in the kitchen, and to walk barefoot in the garden, enjoying this newfound communion.

Seven months into our new marriage, I was pregnant. All I once thought I knew of life and love and God were showered with grace as He whispered, "I will make all things new in you." As new wine burst forth through old wineskins, the ponderings of my heart laid barren before the throne. What I could not comprehend of a God-Head, Three in One, was now powerfully displayed. In our meager attempt of love, Kevin and I had created life held in my body. There was no turn or change where I could deny the presence and truth of it all. He is magnificent. How He longs for us to know Him. *Praise the Lord, Oh my Soul. Let all that is within me . . . Bless the Lord.*[13] I swayed in church, my belly a garden bed.

My dear friend nodded graciously as I clamored for an explanation of my body, no longer mine. *I am one person and two people at the same time.* The thought would not let me go. It persisted in my mind and heart and filled my skin. And so, the relationship continued. What was once two meager souls becoming a ragged portrait of one unified whole is now complete and perfect in the beating heart that lay close to mine. In the quiet of my sanctuary, the words whispered, "You will have a son. His name is Judah."

It was not until my belly was swollen and little feet kicked within that I accepted my new role as mother, a perfect creation of God was alive within me. He breathes life in us, the Beautiful Creator who calls us His own. I participated with Him in this dance, but He always leads. I learned the steps to follow.

I awakened, as usual, heavy with the weight of the child in my womb. Restless. Anxious. In the darkness of night, our son's time had come. I kissed Kevin softly as he slept. He shuffled to his side.

"Are you ready to meet your son?" I whispered.

The next thirty-eight hours proved to be the most vulnerable and submissive hours I had known. Sleep was not an option with the uncertainty of labor. Kevin and I enjoyed the sunshine, laughing and conspiring about the new life we would share. We walked atop the same grass where we stole kisses while dating, where my hand embraced a promise of wedded life, and where vows were made 'til death do us part. Knowing these short months of just the two of us, a newly married couple, were coming to a close left a bittersweet taste. I wanted to sip these husband and wife moments and make them last.

By nightfall, contractions remained steady. I could not find contentment. I wanted to progress. Hand in hand, Kevin and I waited. We prayed. We sang. We lit candles. I longed to meet my baby. I pushed through the contractions, desperate to meet him, yet unaware time was not my own. In the middle of the night, our midwife checked my progress giving me only three to four centimeters of dilation. My heart sank. My body ached. Tiredness crept under my skin, but the pain would not lend way to sleep. I tried to relax and submit my limbs to the warmth of the bath water, but my body would not succumb. With every contraction, I held onto Kevin, allowing his hands to help me. He cried. I cried.

"I'm so proud of you," he encouraged.

He was always reassuring me. As his eyes held mine, an eternal instant suspended time. The magnitude of emotion only became diminished by words. We were truly one. We both knew our lives would never be the same, that marriage matters, and love is enough.

My strength was depleted; there was no tangible end to this labor. My thoughts were scattered and slow. Like Moses, hidden in the cleft of the rock, I waited for God. He did not come in the earthquake, but in a stillness that allowed peace to come to the foreground.

I wept, fears relieved. My hands could not help but lift toward heaven to grasp the unseen stars hidden by the light. This was worship. I stood broken before the Lord, open and ready for Him to be my strength, to deliver this child into my arms. It is His time. Not my own. It was our created mission, unscripted and uncensored.

Dehydration and exhaustion brought physical challenges as I passed out hard on our bed. Opting for a home birth, my determination to remain at home was paramount. At the mention of hospitalization, I tried to regain strength. Increasing my effort was beyond my capacities, so I chose submission so His presence could be made known. I drank in the air as a prayer, and I prayed hard.

The midwife made her round to check Judah's tiny heart,

which remained strong from within. I chose, in the beginning, to push too soon, and his head was stuck sideways inside the curve of my pelvis. Our midwife intervened, lending her hands to maneuver Judah into a better position. Without medication, the pain was excruciating. Every contraction was a desperation that felt like it would last an eternity.

The midwife looked at me sternly. "Christine, you must breathe, or he won't make it. Just breathe."

I had spent my life in this process, learning to breathe. I inhaled slowly, bringing in His spirit, life, and strength. I exhaled my fear. A new sense of determination filled me at the sight of our son's head. Without knowing the day or hour, I came to the end of labor. My body did not betray me. The pain taught me to trust, to know where to lean in, and where to rest. I pushed hard one last time. The fierce lion boy delivered into his Papa's hands, our Judah. More deeply than I knew was possible, I fell in love again with my God, who renewed my strength and opened my eyes to Love, with my beloved husband whose faith in me never wavered, and with my tiny newborn son. My son, whom I loved before I met him, would teach me more about God than a thousand pages could ever contain.

Chapter 13

There are days you walk forward with your partner, hand in hand, and days where you lie in bed, back to back, with a faint disbelief of all the weight and joy. Our reality became an obscured perception in the thick of a new marriage and a child, as gritty in our hands as it was in our hearts. Each morning, I opened my eyes to see the man I married and vowed to love. My existence was to be an ezer—a helper in his despair—a friend, lover, mother to our child, and rib to his side. An almost childlike emotional urgency caused my eyes to stand affixed, craving his gaze, but I was quickly distracted by the flailing arms and smile of the baby boy he held.

Kevin and I deeply longed for a family with laughter and noise. Judah was our daily reminder of our desire for more children. Yet, in my selfishness and tiredness, I did not want to comply. My mind refused to accept the idea of another labor; fear gripped itself tightly around my fingers as I prayed. It was not until I opened my hands to worship that God whispered Ecclesiastes over me:

> *Two are better than one...*
> *If either of them falls down,*
> *one can help the other up.*
> *But pity anyone who falls*
> *and has no one to help them up.*
> *Also, if two lie down together, they will keep warm.*
> *But how can one keep warm alone?*
> *… A cord of three strands is not quickly broken.*[14]

After the glorious revelation of God's gentle nudge, rivers

of conversation and fear were swept aside. In the quiet, my heart began to open and say yes to the potential of a sibling for Judah. Come pain, come labor, come what may—I would endure another labor if it led to a greater capacity for love.

And so it was.

The twinge deep within my belly affirmed my suspicions. It was the same spark I felt with the lion boy as I became pregnant again. Kevin and I held one another close, our eyes wild with wonder at what this next child would bring to us.

A family of four. I laughed in disbelief.

There was a thickness of unknowing and amazement. We stopped immediately to pray. "This is your child. Just as we know with Judah, we are only temporary parents here for a short time. May Your will be done."

Kevin and I found one another's eyes and held them until we could not help but smile at the other's thoughts. Our secret joy pulsed between us. With the holiday excitement compounding our decision to share the news with our family, I wrapped tiny socks underneath the fir tree to make the announcement. Brightly illuminated strands of lights twinkled with hopefulness. As the family gathered in the upcoming weeks, we would introduce the coming of Judah's younger sibling for everyone to rejoice with us during this season of Christmas.

I dreamed of a dark-headed child in the dead of night. Another son. The tiny head rested close to my breast, wrapped in white cloth. My arms felt the weight of this body, and I awakened with immense peace. Kevin and I chose the name Samuel Ransom, and we discussed bunk bed plans for the boys to share.

Two weeks before Christmas, blood ran thick as I collapsed to the floor. Kevin ran to the shower, finding me lying underneath the stream of water. He lifted me to his chest, and I fell hard into him. I wailed, refusing to be comforted. The water poured over my empty body, cleansing the ground. I could not look at him, blurred with the shame of my broken body.

Minutes passed before I was able to utter the words, "Our baby is gone."

Days wasted themselves as I wept them away. *Where is the*

promise of the One they call Faithful? I had spent so much time refuting the Lord over having another child, only to open myself up to His plan and have it destroyed within the same breath. Hope became a tormentor of my despair.

"I know this is hard," Kevin held my face, "but we both know this child was never ours."

I pushed his hands away and shook my head slowly, refusing his words.

Time dripped like honey from the comb. Mothering did not come with personal days. Judah raced around with his sturdy legs and golden wheat hair. I kissed him every second that went by and waited for the pain to ease. He wrinkled his tiny nose with a smile, new teeth pushing through the soft gums. I sat on the floor and let the tears land on the top of his head, smiling when he looked up at me. His eyes, large almonds, lit with the newness of life and love. He laughed. And I laughed with him as tears effortlessly fell.

Finding joy amidst this suffering was a daily act of the will, a choice to accept who I was in light of His mercy. Prayer did not allow an escape from the grief. I pleaded quietly for Christ to walk beside me, behind me, and before me through the thick of it, to somehow allow my faith to be made tangible.

I sat with a group of women I had never met, tied only by the Spirit we chose to accept, binding us into a mysterious sisterhood. We opened the Bible, and I was asked to read aloud:

And the God of all grace, who called you to his eternal glory in Christ, after you have suffered a little while, will himself restore you and make you strong, firm, and steadfast.
1 Peter 5:10 (NIV)

A woman turned the pages of her Bible and landed on the prophet Hosea. She read clearly, the voice of the Almighty strained in my ears:

"Come, let us return to the Lord.

> *He has torn us to pieces*
> *but he will heal us;*
> *he has injured us*
> *but he will bind up our wounds.*
> *After two days he will revive us;*
> *on the third day he will restore us,*
> *that we may live in his presence.*
> *Let us acknowledge the Lord;*
> *let us press on to acknowledge him.*
> *As surely as the sun rises,*
> *he will appear;*
> *he will come to us like the winter rains,*
> *like the spring rains that water the earth."*[15]

And so, those winter rains continued to drive out the sorrow, establishing me in the root system of faithful believers. God slowly taught me of the plans to prosper and not to harm, to give hope and a future.[16] The lion boy reminded me daily that praise belongs to the Lord. As I imagined our child dancing on the other side of eternity, I whispered over myself: *I will wait patiently for the Lord. He will restore me. He will bind up this broken heart. He is faithful. I choose to believe that the most glorious thing is His goodness, which means I have to choose that my body is also still good.*

When night fell, Kevin whispered, "You are beautiful."

As I retreated within myself, he reached his arm around my waist; I took shelter beneath the sheets. The beauty of these scars born of the weight of a child got lost in translation within my husband's tender words. The shame I felt from the heaviness of loss gave way to a vulnerability, widening the gap between what I was and what I ought to be in my mind.

"I'm scared," I finally admitted, stepping out from behind my shame. "I feel like my body is broken, like I am still broken."

Kevin reminded me of who I was as his wife, as his beloved, and as Christine. He invited me into the safety of sharing those fragile thoughts and memories. We found a therapist and a spiritual director and began story-sharing with others who had walked through miscarriage and abuse. We learned how to pray out of a space of deep connection and to love even through our fear. We rewrote our narratives, grieving and reclaiming our life as a partnership. We chose to be there for one another when we wanted to run, hide, and blame.

With each step of openness, I found safety within the healing. I began to reinvent places, songs, dreams, and events that once kept me stuck in a cycle of trauma. Within these circles of community and friendship, I picked up my suitcase and traveled right back into the center of devastation, seeing it with a fresh perspective as it changed me. As someone whose wounds were not as ugly and scary anymore, I traced the lines of my memories, asking God to show up. This became a sacred space on a yoga mat, my prayer rug. My internal landscape began to shift. I walked away from my yoga prayer sessions feeling as though my memory could contain something happier, a little more vibrant to hold onto for the ride into the future.

The day my childhood friend, Anna, called unexpectedly, I knew something had been lost in my stomach. She was weeping and asked me to pray. "It's my mom," she sobbed. "She was hit by a speeding driver. Christine, I don't think she will make it through the night."

We sat on the phone, only our breath between us, silent prayers being uttered.

Death is kindness to some and a torment to most. I found Anna amidst the crowd of dark-colored suits and dresses. Her blonde hair cascaded down to her waist, and she smiled. I hugged her until I became uncomfortable and aware this was not where we wanted to meet again after all these years. We looked into each others' eyes as only childhood friends can, not having to speak a word. We shared a look of knowing. Mom, Dad, Michelle, and April followed behind us as we hugged Anna's siblings and Dad. I turned to find the exit as we said our final condolences. Alex was standing in front of the door with his unmistakable red hair and freckles. My breath caught in my chest, and my legs buckled underneath me. I grabbed Kevin's arm and turned toward the wall, exhaling deeply.

"It's him," I whispered, deepening my face into Kevin's

chest. I held myself there for a breath, reminding myself to feel the weight of gravity beneath me. I took another deep inhalation. *I am no longer the little girl you once knew. You have no power here, other than the power I give you.* I stood up tall, taking hold of Kevin's hand.

"I'm ready to leave," I said firmly.

"Are you okay?" Kevin moved toward the opposite door.

"I am. I really am." I smiled, nodded, and took another step forward.

Our friends planned a trip to the beach, and we willingly joined. I packed our suitcases, and we made our way to a place I told them I had never been before. We settled in, spending our day watching Judah splash in the water. The rays of light grew brighter over the horizon as I scooped up the sandy boy into my arms. Judah rested his head on my shoulder as we stood to leave the ocean. Kevin took hold of my hand as I paused, glancing toward the pier in the distance. A memory began to form, one so deep I almost forgot it was there. I took another step onto the sand, the water continuing to lull in and out with the tides. Like a faded photograph coming into view, a clear picture took shape in my mind. My thoughts began to darken as I looked over the dunes to the left of us.

Kevin looked at me and squeezed my hand a little tighter to spur me toward our hotel. I stand still, transfixed. My feet were buried within the waves that pooled around my ankles. I was sinking.

"That is the place," I said in a vacant tone. My feet were stone. My eyes welled with tears. "This is the place where Derek…" I could not make out the word.

Kevin nodded and looked at me knowingly.

"What happened to you is not your fault, Christine," Kevin said deliberately. "He cannot hurt you again, not unless you let the memory keep you here. You have to choose to forgive if you want to be free."

"I know," I responded. "I just never thought forgiveness would be this difficult."

Kevin continued, "You aren't alone anymore. I love you.

I'm here."

"I love you, too," I replied, hugging Judah a little tighter. I smiled, shifting from reinvention to redemption.

I dove headlong into a community of men and women who gathered around me, holding me each step of healing. I fumbled in and out of depression, questioning the necessity of this trauma work. The woman who led the restoration workshop, where Kevin and I first met, agreed to meet with me. We dusted off the residue of distrust and abuse. Every three steps forward, I stumbled backward. But still, it was progress. My legs began to build beneath me as I breathed a new mantra: *root to rise*. I found my grounding disarming the lies within. I chose to get really low, sink into trusting people again, drink from the depths of Scripture, and learn that my body is a beloved vessel. I began to peel the wax of insincerity from my bones and allow Light to shine through for others to see. I began telling my story, sharing my pain, only to hear the healing words "I'm sorry" and "Me, too." The best of these friendships were sometimes the ones who said nothing. They just remained faithful with quiet perseverance, showing up when I failed to accept the truth in myself repeatedly.

On Easter morning, I drove alone from a Sunday service toward our home, greeting Kevin and Judah with kisses. Hands trembling, I called Kevin into the bedroom. Two lines appeared as we held our breath. Our rainbow baby was here. I imagined our next son, a brother for Judah, to share space and time. Halfway through the pregnancy, my fears were relieved of miscarrying again, and I sank deeply into breathwork preparation for labor. We met with our midwife, who scanned the tiny heartbeat thumping in time with my own rhythm.

"Your daughter's heart is strong," she stated proudly, rubbing the ultrasound wand across the top of my growing belly.

"What?" I asked in disbelief.

"You're having a girl." Her eyes met my wide expression.

Kevin squeezed my hand gently as I fixated on the details of tiny toes, widening fingers, and bubbles floating through the house of my body. He laughed.

I joined in the laughter, tears flowing in a steady stream.

"What are you going to do with another version of me?" I asked Kevin, still shaking with joy.

"Love her," he bent down and kissed me through salted lips.

"I don't want her to have my story," I whispered as the joy momentarily gave way to fear.

"She won't," Kevin reassured me.

"She doesn't even have a name," I sighed.

"We'll wait to meet her. She has a name. We just don't know it yet," Kevin said quietly. He's always teaching me.

It was a clear, cool morning the day I inhaled my daughter's soft, warm skin. I had been teaching her how to breathe ever since. Kevin placed her tiny body on my chest as our lungs recycled air back and forth.

He looked up at me with confidence I had never known from him, "Her name is Josephine."

"Josephine," I exhaled over her. "Josephine Lynn. I love you, my sweet girl. I love you because you are mine."

As I danced with our new daughter, we learned the steps together. This shared humanity and storytelling does not end with me, but carries on into the fabric of the next generation. I dignify my own pain in order to find healing so I can extend the same grace to her. One day, I will share my story with her and invite her to share her own. To be beloved is to be believed. To be beloved is to be loved. In order to love, we must simply learn to be. To breathe. To breathe in love and to exhale it over one another.

As I struggle daily to live up to my new name, the one given to me as a gift of a new covenant, I fight to feel like I belong, to accept that I am known and loved. I fight to not want to peel my skin from the shame of past abuse or drink until all memory fades. I fight to deny the ache under my skin that beckons to be carved out, to rebuke the voice of the lie that hisses: I will never be good enough, strong enough, pretty enough, clean enough, or worthy. The lie that accuses me: *unlovable*.

To rewrite *Beloved* over my soul, I must continue learning

how to breathe again, each inhalation and exhalation, the very life, the very breath, the very name of YHWH that breathes us into existence.

ACKNOWLEDGMENTS

Kevin, whose willingness to enter into my story is the greatest love I have known this side of eternity.

To my son, Judah, for teaching me to find joy in the ordinary.

For my daughter, Josie, whose voice helps me find my own.

Thank you, Autumn, for believing in me when I didn't believe in myself.

To Mrs. Herring, my senior literature teacher, who allowed me to share my personal writing without judgment.

For UHP, for taking a risk on me and validating the broken parts of our stories are also filled with redemption.

To my Uncle Andy, a fellow author, whose wisdom and storytelling inspire me to continue to write.

And to my mother, whose steadfast faith has paved a well-worn path of love and acceptance.

To those unnamed, I am filled with gratitude for all of the text messages, emails, prayers, and encouragement throughout this process.

To the rest of my family, whose roots have built the solid foundation in which I continue to grow, I am humbled.

To my honest and authentic friends, your courage to travel the wilderness is nothing short of brave.

To those who will choose to walk forward and own their stories, you are my heroes.

NOTES

1. Beauty and the Beast, VHS, directed by Gary Trousdale and Kirk Wise, 1991, Hollywood: Buena Vista Pictures, 1992.

2. Fitzgerald, F Scott. The Great Gatsby. Harlow, England: Penguin Books, 2013.

3. Matthew 3:17.

4. Tolkien, J. R. R. The Lord of the Rings. London, England: HarperCollins, 1991.

5. Luke 4:21.

6. Luke 4:18-19.

7. Psalms 46:10.

8. 1 Corinthians 13.

9. John 3:27.

10. Trinity Vineyard. "Prayer of Saint Francis." Spotify. Track 6 on Prayers of the Saints: A Trinity Worship Project. CDBY, 2006, Spotify Audio.

11. Isaiah 61:10, NIV.

12. Mark 10:8.

13. Psalms 103:1-2.

14. Ecclesiates 9:4-12.

15. Hosea 6:1-3.

16. Jeremiah 29:11.

Christine Cown was born in a log cabin built by her father in a small town in Georgia. A former Kids' Pastor, she currently owns Haven Yoga studio in Atlanta. When not practicing yoga or writing, Christine can be found alongside her husband, Kevin, dreaming up new house projects with their two kids, Judah and Josephine. *Breath in Our Lungs* is Christine's first book.

www.ingramcontent.com/pod-product-compliance
Lightning Source LLC
Chambersburg PA
CBHW060524080526
44586CB00012B/604